THE MIRACLE OF LOURDES

THE MIRACLE OF LOURDES

· · · a message of healing and hope

JOHN LOCHRAN

ST. ANTHONY MESSENGER PRESS
Cincinnati, Ohio

Excerpts from *Lourdes: In Bernadette's Footsteps* by Joseph Bordes are used with permission of MSM Editions.

Excerpts from *Les écrits de Sainte Bernadette et sa Voie Spiritulle,* by Andre Ravier, are used with permission of Lethielleux/Meta Editions.

Cover photo and photo on page 43 are used by permission of PhotoViron.

Every effort has been made to trace and acknowledge the copyright holders of all the material excerpted in this book. The editors apologize for any errors or omissions that may remain and ask that any omissions be brought to our attention so that they may be corrected in future editions.

Scripture passages have been taken from *New Revised Standard Version Bible,* copyright ©1989 by the Division of Christian Education of the National Council of the Churches of Christ in the U.S.A., and used by permission. All rights reserved.

Cover and book design by Mark Sullivan

LIBRARY OF CONGRESS CATALOGING-IN-PUBLICATION DATA
Lochran, John.
The miracle of Lourdes : a message of healing and hope / John Lochran.
p. cm.
ISBN 978-0-86716-863-1 (pbk. : alk. paper) 1. Lourdes, Our Lady of. I. Title.

BT653.L63 2008
232.91'7094478—dc22

2007046509

ISBN 978-0-86716-863-1
Copyright ©2008, John Lochran. All rights reserved.

Published by St. Anthony Messenger Press
28 W. Liberty St.
Cincinnati, OH 45202
www.SAMPbooks.org

Printed in the United States of America.
Printed on acid-free paper.
08 09 10 11 12 5 4 3 2 1

contents

*B*etween February 11, 1858, and July 16, 1858, there were eighteen apparitions of Our Lady to Bernadette. The place where Mary appeared was called Massabielle. In the local dialect of the area it means "old rock." On this old rock three churches have been built, each on different levels: the Rosary Basilica, the Upper Basilica of the Immaculate Conception and the crypt or chapel of adoration. Over the years other churches have been built, such as the underground Basilica of Pius X, with a capacity for twenty-five thousand people, and the Church of St. Bernadette, with a capacity for six thousand. Information offices, meeting rooms, baths, fountains and many other amenities have also been added to cater for the huge number of pilgrims. All of these churches and facilities are located in an area of the shrine known as the "Domaine." Within the "old rock" itself is a cave where the actual apparitions took place. Today this cave is known as the Grotto of Lourdes, and it is the central focus for pilgrims to Lourdes. At this Grotto pilgrims gather from around the world. As they gaze upon the statue of Our Lady, in a recess of the rock above them, they are drawn into the story of Lourdes, a story that both encompasses and goes beyond the exchanges that took place between Mary and Bernadette. The story reveals the wider horizon of the Gospels. It is within the gospel perspective that we need to ponder the meetings that took place between the Mother of God and a little peasant girl of the French Pyrenean mountain range, and to hear again the words given by Mary to her. This is what Mary said to Bernadette:

"Would you be so kind as to come here for fifteen days?"
"I cannot promise you the happiness of this world but of the other."

"Penance, penance, penance, pray for the conversion of sinners."

"Go, drink at the spring, and wash yourself there."

"Would you kiss the ground and crawl on your knees for sinners."

"Would you eat the grass that is there for sinners?"

"Go and tell the priests to build a chapel here, and to have people come in pilgrimage."

"I am the Immaculate Conception."[1]

In the reflections that follow, these words will be taken up again and lead us into the heart of the message that is Lourdes—a message of the Gospels.

Lourdes was once described to me as the "Disney World of the Catholic church," as "God's Magic Kingdom." I had to reply that it is the complete opposite. Disney World is a commercial enterprise where joy and pleasure is manufactured and paid for. Lourdes is about generosity of spirit where true joy is found in giving time and loving service freely to the sick and those in need. It has nothing to do with magic or fairy tales and legends. It is founded on reality, a remarkable reality, historical reality, above all a sacred reality.

At the heart of Lourdes stands an encounter of love between a child and a Mother, a child called Bernadette Soubirous and Mary, Mother of God and our Mother. That meeting happened a long time ago in 1858. It was a sacred and special moment that would forever change the face of a small French village, reach way beyond the Pyrenees, reawaken the spiritual yearnings of people from every corner of the earth and make Lourdes what it is today, a worldwide center of pilgrimage.

In 1858, with a population of little more than three thousand, Lourdes was a small unimportant provincial village of the Pyrenees in the southwest of France. The populace was sharply divided between the upper, middle and lower classes. Amongst the poorest of the poor were the Soubirous family. François Soubirous, a miller by trade, his wife Louise and their four children had fallen upon hard times, their ultimate degradation that of being forced to live in a place called the "Cachot," an old jail unfit for human habitation.

Bernadette, at the age of fourteen, shared the family humiliation and their mutual heartache. It was a time of great difficulty and darkness, a time of desolation and almost despair. But heaven was about to have its say.

On Thursday, February 11, 1858, life was to change dramatically for Bernadette, never to be the same. On a cold, damp, miserable day, a simple search for firewood, and the need to find warmth for the body, became instead an amazing encounter with heaven and a love to warm the heart. The last of the firewood had gone. Bernadette, her sister Toinette and friend Jeanne Abadie went off to fetch some. At a rocky recess in a place known as Massabielle, where the river currents washed up driftwood and all kinds of debris, Bernadette had a vision that would leave an indelible imprint on her heart and mark the beginnings of the story that is Lourdes.

In this Grotto she saw a Lady "dressed in white with a blue sash and a yellow rose on each foot, the color of her rosary." Who the "Lady" was became the subject of much debate. There were eighteen apparitions in all, the last one taking place on July 16, 1858.

As news reached the townspeople and neighboring districts, crowds began to flock to the Grotto. With the discovery of a spring of water, and the news of healings taking place, the crowds became ever more numerous. For Bernadette it was a time of private ecstasy and public hell. She was mocked, ridiculed, laughed at by some. A fourteen-year-old, uneducated, illiterate child, she was hounded by police and local authorities, interrogated and even threatened with prison. In the face of all adversity, she remained steadfast. Even the local priest, the Abbé Dominique Peyramale, who was skeptical at first, began to believe her and became convinced when, at the ninth apparition on March 25, the Feast of the Annunciation, the "Lady" herself revealed her identity: "I am the Immaculate Conception." Peyramale knew that a poor, uneducated child with no formal religious training or doctrinal knowledge could ever have invented such a title—a dogma just recently proclaimed by the church in 1854.

After four years of stringent church investigation, the clear evidence of Bernadette's credibility, and thirty-five cases of inexplicable healing, the local bishop, in a pastoral letter dated January 18, 1862, declared: "truly, the Blessed Virgin Mary did appear to Bernadette."

Bernadette remained in Lourdes until 1866 when, at the age of twenty-two, she journeyed to Nevers in the north of France to join the Sisters of Charity and Christian Learning. She was to remain there until her death at the age of thirty-five on April 16, 1879.

The message of Lourdes is a gospel message. In all of the exchanges that took place between Our Lady and Bernadette at Massabielle, Mary calls humanity to rediscover again the Good News that God loves us and cares about us. No matter who we are, Christ is there for us. Lourdes is none other than the gospel message of a Father who in love waits for the return of the prodigal. It is a story of the Son who shows us the way back home, a message of conversion and mission that we may witness to the way of Jesus in the church and in the world. Lourdes is about pilgrimage—the pilgrimage we make through life with God, in God and to God.

Through the years Lourdes has often become synonymous with the physically sick. There is certainly a message of great hope and consolation for the physically sick and disabled. There have indeed been miraculous cures. They are well documented. And we should not be afraid to pray for physical healing. That is an act of faith in a Jesus who came to save the lost and the sick. But the message of Lourdes goes way beyond that of physical healing. Our Lady came especially to bring about in us the healing of the heart. It is here that Jesus wants to touch us most of all—in our hearts. "Our hearts know no rest until they rest in you," said

Saint Augustine. If we can come to the same conclusion, then we will have discovered the true meaning of pilgrimage. For a world so often restless, it is a conclusion we need to discover urgently.

In 1985 I was appointed chaplain in Lourdes for the English-speaking pilgrims and served for ten years. To serve as a chaplain of Our Lady of Lourdes is always an honor for any priest. To me it meant so much more. It was a gracious gift of a merciful and loving God who, in bringing me to Lourdes, gave me new life, new hope and a new mission.

The story of my coming to Lourdes began in a place thousands of miles away from Europe and the Pyrenean Mountains. Indeed, in a most unlikely spot within the heart of an altogether different continent, Africa. As a young missionary priest I had been sent to the Democratic Republic of the Congo. There, as I now realize, the mysterious ways of Divine Providence moved to guide my steps on the path of a personal pilgrimage to Lourdes and a rendezvous with God's healing love.

At the entrance to the mission where I worked in the Congo was a huge statue of Our Lady of Lourdes. I began to notice a poor African stumble his way to that statue day each day. He could barely walk or speak, his arms were completely paralyzed, and his eyes were fixed in some strange trance. (Some members of his tribe had poisoned him in an act of revenge.) My heart was filled with pity as I saw him, day after day, limp along the road toward Mary. Little did I know then that, within a short period of time, I myself would be limping along the road toward Mary, coming before her, broken in body and spirit, to kneel at her feet at the Grotto of Lourdes.

In the Congo I became very ill. It was a sudden and serious illness that worsened each day and spanned a period of two years. Along with physical suffering came a nightmare of pain and frustration, a time of vacillation between hope and almost utter despair. I felt abandoned by the Lord. The future, if there was to be any, looked bleak. It was in this moment of impasse that the Lord in his mercy touched my life. Led by his hand, I found myself in Lourdes before the heart of Mary. Not only was I healed, but also through a whole series of events I came to be chaplain for the English-speaking pilgrims. Such are the wonderful ways of God's mercy.

The year 2008 marks the 150th anniversary of the appearance of Our Lady to Bernadette. One hundred fifty years down the road, the message of this remarkable and moving story is as valid today as it was then. It has touched the hearts and shaped the lives of countless peoples and continues to do so today. Lourdes is a message not just for a past time. It is for our time, for every time.

The reflections I would like to share with you have been written for all those who, like me and my poor African brother, "limp along the road toward God," especially those who are disabled by the burdens of the heart and long to know the tender mercy of God. It was Bernadette who said, "The Grotto was my Heaven."

I hope you will find in these reflections something of that "heaven," something of that deeply personal love that Bernadette experienced and which God wishes to bestow upon us all. I hope they will be a help to you on a pilgrimage to Lourdes and for that longer pilgrimage you make daily toward the heart of the living God.

part i

Lourdes

"The Grotto was my Heaven"

chapter one

• • • SPRINGS OF LIVING WATER • • •

Over the years I have often been asked why such a multitude of people come to Lourdes. It is not an easy question to answer. To have a more comprehensive response you would really need to ask each of the five million or so people who come every year to this shrine. Even then you would probably have five million very different answers. I think people come here because they are thirsty. There is an elemental thirst in the heart of each of us, a thirst for life, for answers to the restless yearnings of our hearts, a thirst for wholeness in body and in spirit, above all a thirst to love and be loved. Lourdes stands like an oasis in the wilderness of our time. It is a place where we can quench that thirst. "Go drink at the spring and wash yourself there," Our Lady said to Bernadette. On one level she points to the physical as she makes known to Bernadette a spring of water. But on another level the Blessed Virgin points us beyond the physical to the spiritual. We see that this is no mere water. It is the symbol of Jesus himself. He is the living water.

We do not have to believe in apparitions, in any apparitions (although in the case of Lourdes I believe you would be a fool if you didn't). We are not obliged to, since they are not essential to our faith. What is so great about Lourdes is that it always brings us back to what is essential. The Blessed Virgin always points us in the direction of the Gospels. She always points us, under the guidance of the Holy Spirit, to Jesus her son who in turn reveals to us the Father's love. In Lourdes there are many processions and ceremonies. However, Lourdes is much more than this. It is much more than a place of devotion, more than a place of physical healing. It is above all a place in which we rediscover from the heart of God how much God loves us, how much we are held in God's mercy.

One day in a little office I had within the shrine the door suddenly burst open. A lady stood there, an Indonesian woman from Singapore, who clearly was very ill. "What must I do to be healed?" she blurted out. My first instinct was to say that there was no magic formula, that there was no special ritual that led to some automatic cure. I was about to say this but thankfully did not. Just for a moment there was a grace-filled pause, and I found myself being transported to that well-known scene of the Gospel in which the rich man approaches Jesus and asks: "[W]hat must I do to inherit eternal life?" (Mark10:17). What the lady from Singapore was asking was no different. She wanted life. We all do. Consciously or subconsciously, we are always searching for happiness, for peace, for wholeness, for healing.

In the shrine of Lourdes, today as yesterday, multitudes gather just like those who gathered around Jesus on the hills of Galilee hungry not for "bread alone," but for "every word that comes from the mouth of God" (Matthew 4:4). Every year people come from every corner of the earth, people of every creed and color. Many come just to see, to visit. Not everyone comes to pray. Lourdes can also be a world of superstition, simple tourist curiosity and religious commerce of the worst kind. But many more people do come to Lourdes thirsting for the answer to the burdens and anxieties that afflict their lives and trouble their spirits.

Like the woman from Singapore, many do come in search of physical healing, and why not? I remember once, while on holiday at home in my native Scotland, I went into the local church to pray. I happened upon a group of people clearly about to set off on pilgrimage to Lourdes. Their priest was saying to them: "Now, don't be going to Lourdes looking for miracles of healing." I understood where the priest was coming from. He was afraid their prayers might not be answered and they would come home disappointed. But it was the wrong approach. The true Christian approach is to believe that with God all things are possible— to pray by all means for the miracle and at the same time to pray to accept and live whatever God allows.

The God we believe in is the God of the impossible. Lourdes is a credible witness to this belief. Numerous claims of healing have been investigated throughout its history. Since its beginnings in 1858, after stringent investigations, some sixty-five or so cases of physical healing have been declared medically and scientifically inexplicable and recognized by the church as miraculous. For whatever genuine reason one comes to Lourdes, for healing of the body or wholeness of the spirit, no one, on the whole, leaves disappointed. Even those who come for physical healing and do not find it often leave with a realization that beyond all the pain and darkness of our lives there is a love that holds us together.

"Hell is not to suffer; hell is to suffer without love," a pilgrim once told me in Lourdes. Hell is indeed the agony of being without love. Lourdes speaks of heaven, not hell, and reminds us of a love that is always there to hold us. For the sick and the disabled, Lourdes becomes a school in which to learn to surrender and abandon our lives and hearts into the hands of God. We have to learn to trust God enough to allow him to create a new and better life even from the worst of circumstances. Many people say to the sick, "Offer up your suffering to God." That sentiment can conjure up a narrow and mean image of God. How can the one who loves us so much be happy to receive the morbid gift of our unhappiness? What we can offer to God is not so much our sufferings in themselves, but the patience and the love with which we try to live with them. In this way our faith in God's providence, and surrender to God's will, may grow.

Many years ago, as I have alluded to in the introduction to this book, I had a very difficult and trying time in my own life. I'd come back from the missions in Africa very ill and could have died. One day in the hospital a young nurse handed me a cassette player, saying, "Here, Father, here's some music for you to cheer you up." The music was a song by an English singer called Elkie Brooks. She was famous in Britain in the 70s and 80s. The song was called "Fool If You Think It's Over." That's just exactly how I was thinking at the time—that it was very much over. I was a fool. Little did I know then that life, far from being over, was just about to begin. I came to Lourdes, was healed and, as they say, the rest is history!

Fool if you think it's over. That was the message given by the Risen Jesus to two very discouraged and downhearted disciples he met on the road to Emmaus. With the death of Jesus all their hopes and dreams had been shattered. He met them on the road of their sorrow and said, "Oh, how foolish you are, and how slow of heart to believe all that the prophets have declared! Was it not necessary that the Messiah should suffer these things and then enter into his glory" (Luke 24:25–26). Jesus didn't come into this world to teach us how to die. He came to teach us how to live in this world and beyond.

"We are an Easter people, and our song is alleluia," said Pope John Paul II. Nowhere is that more evident than in Lourdes. There are people who come in sadness and despair. They often leave with new hope, new heart and new life. Here is a place where truly "the blind receive their sight, the lame walk…the deaf hear" (Matthew 11:5). Not just in physical terms, but especially in the realm of the heart.

Lourdes lies in a mountain valley. The surrounding countryside speaks of fresh pastures, of sheep and of shepherds. We are reminded of Bernadette, the little shepherdess. We are reminded of Jesus, of the words of the book of Revelation: "[H]e will guide them to springs of the water of life" (Revelation 7:17b).

chapter two

• • • SIGN LANGUAGE • • •

*L*ong ago "God spoke to our ancestors in many and various ways through the prophets, but in these last days he has spoken to us by a Son..." (Hebrews 1:1–2).

God speaks a word and the world comes into being. He speaks a word through the prophets and reveals himself to his people. Finally he speaks the last word, the Word that is Jesus. He reveals all he is, and all we are called to live, in the person of his own son. "[T]he Word became flesh and lived among us" (John 1:14). We believe in a God who speaks. His word is an invitation to existence, to dialogue, to communion. Sometimes we don't hear that word. And since we don't hear it, we cannot enter into dialogue or communion. We are like the deaf and dumb, unable to hear, unable to speak, not in the physical sense but in the depths of our hearts. God knows our disabilities. He doesn't leave us in our deafness or our dumbness. In the many and various ways that he speaks, he gives us another language to use, the only one the deaf and the dumb can understand: sign language!

The message of Lourdes comes to us in many signs: The more important are poverty, rock, cave, water and light. They are all outward signs of a deeper spiritual reality that God wishes to work in our hearts. They are great signs, powerful signs that can communicate to us an ever-deeper understanding of the message. But for that to take place, they have to be understood within the context of the Bible and especially the Gospels. Let's take a closer look at these signs:

Poverty is the first sign. On February 11, 1858, it is poverty that forces Bernadette to leave home in search of firewood. It is poverty that brings her to Massabielle and to a "young lady" who waits for her. Bernadette is one of the poor and oppressed that Scripture proclaims are the objects of God's favor and concern.

It was poverty—need—that led the Samaritan woman to fetch water in the desert at Jacob's well, and there Jesus waited for her.

It was poverty that led the Israelites through the desert as they searched for the Promised Land. It is in that desert that God waits for them and with them makes an alliance.

This is the spirituality of the desert. God offers presence and friendship to those who wander poor and in need through the desert of the world in search of life.

Rock is the second of the signs. At the foot of the Pyrenean Mountains, in a cave in the rock known as Massabielle, a lady, enveloped in light, appears, smiles and enters into dialogue with Bernadette. Pilgrims who come to Lourdes stand and pray before this cave where Mary appeared. Daily they kiss and touch the rock where she made herself known to Bernadette. Often they do not comprehend all of the deeper meaning.

The mountain, the rock, the cave is a powerful biblical sign. God is the rock of Israel, the one upon whom the people can rely (Psalm 18:31). He provides water for a thirsty people from the rock of Mt. Horeb (Exodus 17:6) The *rock* is a symbol of the safety, security and fidelity of God: "The LORD is my rock, my fortress" (Psalm 18:2).

The *mountain* is the place where God dwells (Exodus 19; 1 Kings 19). It is the place where he reveals himself. His temple in Jerusalem is built on the mountain and dominates the city.

The *cave*, the grotto, is the heart of the mountain where, in biblical times, the divine presence would make itself known. In the Bible Moses and Elijah are admitted into intimacy with God as they find themselves in a cave.

In Lourdes Mary now replaces the prophets. She is the first witness of the incarnation. She appears in a cave to remind us that the Word was made flesh and dwells among us. Jesus, born in a cave at Bethlehem, reveals himself to humankind.

Water is the third sign. For many who come to Lourdes it is the only sign. Sadly, it is perhaps the least understood. There are people who can go to the baths as many as six times in one day. (We know cleanliness is next to godliness, but that's pushing it a bit too far.) I remember a little boy who went into the children's baths and started screaming, "She's not my mama!" Nine women had pretended to be the boy's mother so they could get into the baths before anyone else. I even heard the story of a farmer giving his pigs Lourdes water to drink so they wouldn't get sick. This is just nonsense. Not only is it not Christian—it is downright pagan. This is what happens when we do not understand what the symbolism of this water means. When we don't understand, we run the risk of falling into superstition and magic.

All kinds of scientific studies have been made on this water. The results of these tests show the water to be just that: There are no special properties, no special healing agents. It's just pure, simple water. The water itself is not miraculous. If the water was miraculous in itself, then anyone and everyone who touched this water would be healed. In that case there would be no need of faith—in God or in anything else. It is not the water that heals—only God heals. God may use the water, but it is only God who heals. It is true that many of the recognized cures of Lourdes have been associated with the water. But people have also been healed in other circumstances: during the processions, while receiving communion, while on the train or plane going home. Some have even been healed a few days after the pilgrimage while at home. In other words, there is no one element that heals. God alone heals. In all these elements the one common factor is God. Consider the Gospel story of the cripple who is lying near the pool of Beth-zatha (John 5). He complains to Jesus that he has no one to put him in the water when it moves, for it is only when the water moves that healing takes place. God moves the water, then comes the healing. So it is with the water of Lourdes. It is only when God touches the water that healing comes about.

To really understand the meaning of this sign, we have to see it in a biblical context and within the context of the wider message of Lourdes that goes beyond the physical to the spiritual. Lourdes speaks of the healing of the heart more than of the body. So, too, does the Bible.

We are reminded of the "living water" promised to the Samaritan woman (John 4:10–14), and to all those who are thirsty (John 7:37). The water that is a sign of the permanent reality of our baptism and of life in the Holy Spirit (John 7:38–39). The whole meaning of the water is about moving away from sin and finding new life in Jesus: "Which is easier, to say to the paralytic, 'Your sins are forgiven', or to say, 'Stand up and take your mat and walk'?" (Mark 2:9). While Jesus is interested in the whole person, both body and spirit, the sign of the water is much more about the spirit than it is about the body.

Light is the fourth sign. On Sunday, February 28, at the end of the twelfth apparition, Bernadette feels a need to leave something of herself at the Grotto. She leaves the candle she has been holding. It was the first of many in a long series as, day after day, year after year, pilgrims leave candles burning at the Grotto. They are little flames but with a very profound meaning. They are signs of faith and of Christian prayer. We are reminded of the Paschal candle, itself a sign of the Risen Christ. We are reminded of the tongues of flame at Pentecost (Acts 2:13), the burning bush of Moses (Exodus 3). Above all, we are reminded of Jesus, "the light of the world" (John 8:12).

We are reminded also of the mission given to each one of us by Jesus: "You are the light of the world." Each evening the procession in Lourdes ends with the words: "You are the light of the world, go carry the light to your brothers." We are light? It can't be serious. We, with all our dark past and sinful present, are light? Are we any better than others? No, we are not. We are just earthen vessels like everyone else. But there is a difference. We are earthen vessels who carry a treasure. The treasure is the word of whom we are servants. We cannot confuse the vessel with the treasure. We cannot equate that word to our own limited vision. We cannot water it down to accommodate the world. Nor can we keep it for ourselves as if it was our own property. We cannot hide the light under the bushel.

Bernadette was a simple, poor girl chosen by Our Lady to go and give a message to the world. We are chosen also. We each have a role to play. When we pass from one country to another, we find at the border signs asking, "Do you have anything to declare?" Sometimes fear and compromise with the world prevent us from "declaring." Bernadette had her fears and her world also to contend with, but another power gave her the courage and the strength to give the message she was asked to give: "There was something in me that helped me overcome the obstacles. I was pressed on all sides but never overcome." That's what she said. It is a strength promised to all of us by Jesus: "[D]o not worry beforehand what you are to say; but say whatever is given to you at that time, for it is not you who speak, but the Holy Spirit" (Mark 13:11). We do not need to stop at the frontiers of fear and pressure from the world. We have much to declare.

We are marked with another sign—the *sign of the cross*. It is not a sign of defeat but of victory. It was the first gesture made by Bernadette and Our Lady at the first apparition, a sacred sign that led them into communication and communion. For we who are Christians, the sign of the cross is the greatest sign language we possess. When we make the sign of the cross, we know with whom we travel, whose word we can trust and share with others, and we know where we are going. We know the sign. Perhaps we just need to learn to speak the language in a better and deeper way.

chapter three

••• WHEN THE SPIRIT MOVES •••

A cold, somber dawn heralded the arrival of February 11, 1858. Dark clouds hung heavy in the sky over Lourdes. The inclemency of the day was not confined to the weather. Dark clouds hung heavy upon a child's heart. Sickness, suffering, poverty, destitution, these were the more hostile elements that clouded Bernadette's life. It was a time of impasse, dead ends and heavy burdens. We all know the feeling. We all have days like this. Sometimes the days stretch into months, sometimes even years. We reach the crossroads of impossibility, situations that lie heavily upon us with no apparent hope of solution. For Bernadette life had come to this. Humanly speaking this was the end of the road. By herself she could not find the way forward. By herself she could not create new life. That can only come from someone greater than we are.

And come it did. On that day of February 11, 1858, Bernadette and some friends went in search of firewood and reached the place known as Massabielle. Here there was a rocky recess where the currents of the local River Gave washed up driftwood. Bernadette was about to cross the River Gave when she heard "a sound like a rush of wind." Words reminiscent of Pentecost, words that announced to the apostles the arrival of the dynamic, life-giving, transforming power of the Holy Spirit. Words from the lips of Bernadette that heralded the presence of that same Spirit and the arrival of the Blessed Virgin Mary.

Dead situations need the breath of the spirit to bring new life. In the chaos of Bernadette's life the Spirit moves. Light begins to dispel the darkness. Heaven embraces earth and the whole of Bernadette's life is changed, and a world of new possibilities opens up. Poverty and sickness remain in her life. The apparitions do not change this. What changes is how it is all lived. In the hands of the Spirit, the way of poverty and suffering become the fertile ground of an ever-deepening journey in the ways of Jesus and holiness of heart. In the hands of the Spirit, Bernadette's life will take on a new direction. In the dynamic power of the Holy Spirit the small village of Lourdes will flourish and become what it is today, a place of hope and prayer for the many who come from all over the world.

We live in an age of great anguish. Many traditional values have broken down both in the church and in society. A church that once was a model of orthodoxy, respect and sound principles has been seriously shaken in a series of sex scandals that have weakened the trust of its members. Politicians can often act recklessly and without integrity, leading us into unnecessary pursuits and even more tragically into wars that destroy lives and depress spirits. Marriage is seen as outdated, divorce remains common, and young people opt for cohabitation rather than commitment. Authority and institutions that yesterday gave guidance and direction are today rife with division or constantly questioned. The plurality of ideas and opinions that abound in society and in the church can leave us confused. We are unsure of the road before us. We are often in a dilemma as to whose authority we can accept. While renewal is vital, relativity can easily be fatal. When there is no reference other than our own limited selves, life can easily degenerate into chaos. In the age of the in-depth analysis, we criticize and question, bisect and trisect. We have much to discuss but few solutions to offer. We are often left with nothing to hold onto. We throw out certain principles and structures but have nothing to offer by way of replacement. All of which tends to make us feel bewildered and very alone as we face the complexities of modern life. Yet this very bewilderment and isolation, instead of leading to despair and discouragement, can become for us a springboard to a new and more authentic living of the Christian message. For it is only when we are poor that the Spirit comes to us. If we truly accept our poverty, our littleness, our sense of helplessness, then we can begin to open our hearts to the presence of the Spirit. More readily we can depend on the Sprit to heal us and to guide us.

Before the empty tomb Mary Magdalene weeps. She weeps not because Jesus is dead. She weeps because she cannot find him; she doesn't know where they have put him. Today we can easily weep with her when we look around our church and wonder where they have put the Spirit of Jesus. Some time ago, when discussing the question of how bishops were elected, a leading prelate in the church said to me: "Well, you know how it is today; it's all about having the right connections!" The right connections, he meant, were people of power and influence. Poor me. I had always thought that the only right connection was the presence of the Holy Spirit filling the heart of a man to live the message of the Gospels and making it clear to all concerned that the choice of God was upon him. The Holy Spirit, the Father of the Poor, cannot be present where poverty is not present. As soon as we love power and position more than the truth, the Holy Spirit can do nothing with us. The Holy Spirit will do everything for us only if we cry out in our need. Only when we cry out our fundamental hunger to love and to be loved will the Spirit lead us into true love, into a real and deep experience of the Father. In the beginning of creation it is the Spirit who moves over the "formless void and chaos" of Genesis 1 and brings order and life. Only the Spirit can bring order from the chaos within our own hearts and around us, within our society and within the church.

Pentecost as described in the Acts of the Apostles is a dramatic pivotal event in the lives of the close disciples of Jesus. In that moment the apostles receive the Holy Spirit in a special way. However while Pentecost is a singular event directly concerning the circle of the twelve, the gift of the Spirit is not confined to this moment. It is offered and given to all who follow Jesus: "I will not leave you orphaned…. [T]he Holy Spirit, whom the Father will send in my name, will teach you everything, and remind you of all that I have said to you" (John 14:18, 26). The Holy Spirit is not a gift reserved to those claiming adherence to the charismatic renewal. It is a gift given in baptism and confirmation to all followers of Jesus. It is a gift given to enable us to live our Christian lives. We sometimes see that life as impossible to live or only for saints. How can we really love our enemies? How can we bless those who persecute us? How can we love one another as Jesus loved us? How can we possibly be compassionate as the heavenly Father is compassionate?

Jesus does not invite us to do something and then not provide the power or the strength to do so. If he invites us to live faithfully the message of the Gospels, then he will make us capable of doing so. If he invites us to be compassionate as the Father is compassionate, then he will empower us to live this reality, to live and love with the tenderness of the Father's heart. It is the same for all that Jesus asks of us. He will empower us. We will be "clothed with power from on high" (Luke 24:49). That is the gift of the Spirit promised by the Father. The Holy Spirit mobilizes all our strength, all our energy and all our capacities toward the goal of contemplating God and toward the good of our neighbors.

Even in our worst moments, those times of utter desolation and impossibility, in those moments when prayer seems an empty gesture, it is "the Spirit [who] helps us in our weakness…[who] intercedes with sighs too deep for words" (Romans 8:26). He is given to empower us to live our questions and complexities in the light of faith, to lead us through the hostile deserts of our troubled existence, to see that we are not at the mercy of events but always within the divine mercy. "How will this come about?" a troubled Mary asks the angel at the annunciation. "The Holy Spirit will come upon you," is the answer (Luke 1:35). We may not know how things will work out in our lives. We may not know the final outcome of our problems or where it's all leading. But the promise remains: "I will not leave you orphaned…" If we cry out in our need, if in our poverty and helplessness we abandon ourselves to the spirit, he will "come upon us" to enlighten us and direct us, to make clear the path before us.

Bernadette was a true child of God. In the poverty and cry of her heart, the Spirit moved to lead her forward on the journey to greater intimacy with the Father. "When we cry, 'Abba! Father!' it is that very Spirit bearing witness with our spirit that we are children of God" (Romans 8:15–16). Today, as we begin to discover our radical need, our immense poverty, today in the impossibilities of our own lives, let us feel the movement of the Spirit in us that make us cry out:

> Our Father, may I today experience the heaven of love where you dwell;
> may your name be sanctified and glorified in all my being and especially in this trial I am suffering;
> may your kingdom come! May Jesus who revealed your kingdom become incarnate in all my difficulties.
> May your will be done in all my pain on earth as it is in heaven!
> Give me today my daily bread, the daily bread of your compassion, the daily bread that is a solution to my problems.
> Forgive me all my sins, especially those that have led me to this situation and forgive all those who by their sinful actions have also made me dwell in darkness;
> and lead us not into temptation, the temptation to discouragement, to despair, to walking away from your heart;
> but deliver us from the evil one, from his lies, from his deceit
> (see Luke 11).

Abba! Father! Send us the Spirit of Love, the Father of the Poor, the giver of all consolation.

chapter four

• • • In the Name of the Father... • • •

*B*efore the unknown we are afraid. Before an unknown "young lady" who had suddenly materialized before her eyes, Bernadette was afraid. Her fear made her reach for her rosary beads. Her hands trembled as she tried to make the sign of the cross. When she finally succeeded she said that she began to feel at ease, that all the fear had left her. Why? Because in making the sign of the cross she invokes Father, Son and Holy Spirit, the Trinity, a community of love in whom there is no fear. So the first meeting between Mary, Mother of God, and a child of a little French village is marked with the sign of the cross. The encounter is firmly initiated, sealed and embraced in the name of Father, Son and Holy Spirit.

The Trinity is a world of relationships, a world of love. It is about divine love, a perfect love, a love greater and so vastly above us. Yet it is at the same time a love not so far above us as to exclude us. Indeed it is the opposite. In the Trinity we are all very much included and passionately loved. We have a Father who so loved the world that he sent his only Son. We have a Son who left the glory of heaven to experience the limitations of the human condition, who suffers and dies to tell us how much we are loved. We have the Holy Spirit given us that we may live fully the teachings of the Son and go further into the mystery of love that is God.

Our belief in the Trinity may be a doctrine and a mystery difficult to explain, even beyond our fullest comprehension, but the reality of it is written, not just in every page of Scripture, but even within the flawed, imperfect world of our own relationships. Every time we love, however flawed, however imperfect that love may be, we reflect something of the Trinity, for where there is love there is God.

That the beginning of the apparitions of Our Lady to Bernadette should be signed and sealed with *the* Christian symbol that is the cross speaks clearly of the providential hand of God, for it encapsulates the very substance of the message of Lourdes: the call made by the Blessed Virgin Mary for humanity to return, to renew and to refresh itself once more within the love of Father, Son and Holy Spirit and to find in this one love that is God, the deeper way of living all our other loves.

In a television interview, when asked what I would say to skeptics, to those who have doubts about the story and message of Lourdes, my reply was that given by Bernadette to the people of her own time: "My job is just to give you the message. It's up to you whether you believe it or not." Whether we believe or not is indeed for us to decide. This is the freedom that God gave us, and God respects that freedom. God imposes nothing. Perhaps our real problem is not so much in believing this or that message or not, but in hearing the message in the first place.

"Would you be so kind as to come here?" These were the words of Our Lady to Bernadette at the third apparition. They are strikingly courteous and homely words. Not command but invitation, not order but request, not imposition but entreaty…an invitation to leave everything else aside and come spend time with Mary. Bernadette was free to accept or reject the request. Of course, who could ever refuse such an invitation from Our Lady? Would we, given such a request, ever dream of refusing it? Of course we wouldn't. Yet we do, and often. The appeal made to Bernadette is one made to us daily. Time and time again the Lord calls to each of us, "Would you be so kind as to come here?" "Would you leave everything else aside and just be with me?" It is the invitation to prayer, to enter the world of God's heart. It is a constant invitation. In all kinds of ways, both subtle and blunt, we manage to ignore it or not to hear the request at all. For we are busy people. Too busy with ourselves to think of the "Father's affairs" (see Luke 2:49). Too busy being the Lord ourselves to allow someone else to be the center of attention. Too busy dreaming of life elsewhere to live it differently now. Too busy with the pleasures and profits of the world to discover the "one pearl of great value" (Matthew 13:45).

No, it is not easy to pray. Talking to God, listening to God's voice, focusing on God is not easy at all. The reality that is God is not like the physical tangible world around us. So we prefer to stay within the limits of our own familiar landscape, the world of those with whom we can be physically present, our family, our friends. Yet our everyday routine reality is never enough; it does not satisfy. Just look at the number of sci-fi programs on television and you realize that we are always on the lookout for something more. One in particular called "Above and Beyond" just about sums it up. It is Jesus who will tell us where the "more" is to be found, and that the "above and beyond" of what we are searching for is really in our midst.

The call to prayer is central to the message of Lourdes. "Pray," Mary said to Bernadette. Their immediate encounter is lived in the praying of the rosary. In the image of Mary and Bernadette together at the grotto we see the "stuff" that prayer is made of. Not the babbling of "empty phrases" that Jesus condemned, but an encounter between two hearts. It is a real prayer that goes beyond the mere recitation of word to become a union of two people held in an embrace of love. This is the prayer we are called to live. Not prayer for the saints alone, but for everyone. Not blind submission to a remote, omnipotent power or a vain search for an unknown God. What is offered is the humble quest of a God who, in the person of Jesus, comes to reveal the love of the Trinity and beg our love in return.

Prayer is being plunged into this community of love that is the Trinity, where, surrounded by love, we feel at home. Prayer is not so much what we have to give to God, but is more a living with God, a "meeting of one friend with another," a personal relationship in which it is truly God who does the giving, the giving of himself for us poor sinners.

"How happy I was, Oh good mother, to have the grace to gaze upon you," Bernadette said in reflecting upon her time spent with the Blessed Virgin.[1] True prayer is this constant gazing, this looking upon, this being with, this faithful contemplation of the beauty and goodness of God that Bernadette experienced.

We are told so many times in the Gospels that Jesus left the crowds behind, went off to a lonely place to pray or spent the night in prayer. What about all the people waiting to be healed, consoled, encouraged and guided? Why does he leave them to go and pray, to be with his Father? Because it is from the prayer that everything else flows. Everything flows from the powerful relationship of love Jesus has with the Father and the Spirit. Prayer is the source of all—of his healing, his compassion, his gentleness, his peace, his understanding. Prayer will bring us also within that same powerful current of love. "My weapons," said Bernadette, "are prayer and sacrifice, and I will hold onto them until my very last breath. In that moment, finally, the weapon of sacrifice will fall away, but the weapon of prayer will follow me to heaven where it will be more powerful than in this land of exile."[2]

We live in a world that has become more competitive, harder, violent, ruthless, cold and impersonal. It is a world that has little room for softness, tenderness and compassion. The workplace, the home, even the church can be so at times. That is why prayer is also so important. We cannot come before the heart of a God of warmth and tenderness and remain an iceberg. In prayer God's love will melt away the hardness. We cannot bring people to God in prayer and remain the same about them. Prayer makes us more thoughtful, more sensitive, more caring.

To find ourselves with God in a heart-to-heart encounter, to love and allow ourselves to be loved. This is the secret of every Christian open to the Good News of Jesus Christ. The secret of all who say yes to the gentle appeal, "Would you be so kind as to come here?"

When we answer that request, we will experience as Bernadette did that we are embraced within that sacred community of love that is Father, Son and Holy Spirit.

chapter five

• • • IN SEARCH OF THE PRODIGAL • • •

A winter's night at the Grotto. My eyes wandered from the statue of Our Lady to the cold, hard, frozen ground below. "Would you be so kind as to kiss the ground for sinners?" I remembered Mary had said this to Bernadette during the ninth apparition. "What sinners?" I wondered. Those of Bernadette's time? Certainly. But then Mary wasn't bound by space and time as we are. The thought suddenly struck me that maybe Bernadette had kissed the ground for me. That maybe she had made this sacrificial act of love for all the people, all sinners who come in pilgrimage to Lourdes. It was a humbling thought.

As I looked up at the Grotto, I thought of another cave, a cave that served as a stable in Bethlehem. I thought of another child who came to "kiss the ground for sinners." Wasn't it exactly this that Jesus had done in leaving all the glory of heaven to bind himself to our earth, to embrace the "ground" that is humanity? Didn't he come to bring a kiss of life to the sick, the lost, the sinful and to embrace us forever in his love?

"Holy Mary, Mother of God, pray for us sinners." We describe ourselves as "sinners," not children or friends, or servants, or the faithful, but sinners. We *are* sinners. We have no difficulty in admitting it. Even those of no religious persuasion do so. Just look at the people so ready to confess their sins on television, radio, in magazines and newspapers. Great is the human need to tell its sins. The telling seems to provide a kind of liberation, an assurance of paying our debts, of expiating and exorcising our woes and clearing our consciences, as if the admission alone can bridge the gap between right and wrong, between sinner and God. But this is not the nature of reconciliation announced by the Gospel. It is not that of being paid for or achieved by our own means. Rather, it is a gift freely given by God in Jesus Christ who bestows upon us a pardon we have no right to merit.

"Kiss the ground for sinners." In Lourdes much of my work took place in the Chapel of Reconciliation hearing confessions. "That must be a very boring job," I was told during the course of a TV interview. I looked upward to heaven for the answer and the answer came: "As it says in Scripture, there is joy in heaven over one sinner who repents. Since I share in the joy of heaven that can never be boring!" The joy of the confessor is indeed that of heaven over one sinner who repents. His sadness is to see hearts that no longer know what real sin is. Real sin is of a deeper nature than a simple admission of weakness. It is to recognize that behind our studied lists of faults and failings there is a deeper sin—our radical incapacity to love. It is only when we make that discovery that we can truly say with the prodigal: "Father, I have sinned against heaven and before you" (Luke 15:18).

The place chosen by Our Lady to appear to Bernadette, the place known as Massabielle, was a rocky recess where the river washed up all kinds of driftwood, refuse, rubbish and debris. It was also a pigsty. It is a reminder of the refuse and rubbish that surface on the shores of humanity, of the violence, hatred, injustice and oppression of our world, of the selfishness that dwells in our hearts. But it is also a reminder of the forgiveness and mercy God holds out to us. A pigsty conjures the image of the Prodigal Son, who, having squandered everything, ends up with the pigs. In the Gospel story we are told that he came to his senses. He recognized his utter misery and saw he was better off in his Father's house. It is only when we come to our senses that true conversion begins to take place. Recognition of our own radical weakness is the only way we will come to feel our utter need of God's help. Only when we are fundamentally convinced that we cannot grow without the love of a caring Father can we begin our return toward him.

Yet even our admission of sin can become itself an obstacle on the road of our return. Sometimes we are like Adam in the garden. Having sinned and having become ashamed of his nakedness, Adam runs to hide from God. When we are confronted with our sins and failures, we fear an angry God in search of reprisal. We stop at our sin; we fear God; we do not wish to appear naked before him, found with our ugliness. We are blocked by a despairing kind of pride that believes God could never love such sinful people. Stopping at our sin, we lose all sight of God's compassion and fail to grasp the very heart of the Good News that we are already forgiven on the cross, that God loves us not because *we* are good but because *God* is good, that Jesus came not for the righteous but for sinners, not to condemn but to enter into the very wounds of our hearts to heal and bring new life.

In life we have a passion for many things, for riches, for pleasure, for position, for power. We have a love of passion. In Jesus, it is utterly different. Not a love of passion but a passion of love. On one of my confessionals in Lourdes I used to have a poster. It was the image of a very simple cross. Underneath were written the words: "It wasn't the nails that held Jesus to the cross but his love for you and me." It is this passion of love that leads Jesus to the extreme, to lay down his life for us. It is the most radical attempt of all by God to convince us that he loves us. But we take some convincing!

At the ninth apparition, hence right at the center of the eighteen apparitions, Mary and Bernadette highlight again this radical love of Jesus. It was during this apparition that Our Lady asked Bernadette to "kiss the ground for sinners," and to undertake other penitential gestures on behalf of sinners. "Would you be so kind as to crawl on your knees for sinners," she said, "to eat the grass that is there for sinners?" When the ninth apparition was taking place, it was Holy Week in Lourdes. So all the gestures that Bernadette makes are an imitation of the passion.

Kissing the ground for sinners reminds us of Jesus embracing humanity in a kiss of life on the cross. Crawling on the ground, of the times Jesus falls to the ground under the weight of the cross. Eating the grass recalls the eating of bitter herbs—the Passover meal of the sacrificial lamb. We are reminded of a God who pursues us in every way even to the point of laying down his life.

Like the father who sees his Prodigal Son "far off," he rushes to meet us, not to condemn or rebuke, not to treat us as our sins would merit, but rather to give us the best, not condemnation, but celebration, for the one who "was dead and has come to life; he was lost and is found" (Luke 15:32).

"Pray for the conversion of sinners," Mary said to Bernadette. The real miracle that Lourdes proposes to us, more than that of the body, is that of the heart, that of our conversion, and the only miracle that requires our cooperation!

Mary calls us not to be afraid of the sin that fills our heart, to turn back to God in spite of our weaknesses. The message of Lourdes calls us not to be afraid of the anguish and guilt we have in not loving enough, but rather to place it where it belongs, before the heart and within the hands of Christ.

What was once a rubbish dump, once a pigsty, is now a place known for God's presence, a place of prayer, caring and brotherhood. This is what God wishes to do with our hearts: to transform us, to heal us of our darkness, to recreate us in his image. Mary points us to the heart of the Gospel, God in search of the prodigal to bring him back home.

chapter six

••• IN A CAVE BY A RIVER…ON THE ROADS WHERE WE WALK •••

Several years ago I said Mass in Lourdes for a group of young people from Kenya. Having been a missionary there, I thought I would use something from that culture as a way of explaining the message of Lourdes. I spoke to them about certain caves found in Zanzibar, caves used during the time of the slave trade as holding pens for those awaiting deportation. Speaking to them about the physical slavery these caves symbolized, I explained how Mary had appeared in a cave, the grotto, to tell us of an even greater slavery, that of sin, and of the Lord's desire to bring us freedom.

At the end of the Mass came the amazing surprise. Just before coming to Lourdes, these young people had made a visit to those very caves in Zanzibar. They had no difficulty in grasping the message of my words. Some may say this was all a coincidence, but I saw clearly the hand of God in these events, an amazing example of Divine Providence. God had prepared these young people for the message God had prepared me to give.

Yet we think that God does not speak to us in the concrete circumstances of our lives! We have neither ears to hear nor eyes to see. Rooted in blindness and indifference, slavishly held by the world around us, we fail to see the hand of God in our midst. That is one of the reasons why the apparitions of Our Lady to Bernadette are so important, for they tell us that God is not confined to heaven or the temple. God is not held within the walls of our churches, but is there out on the roads we walk.

When Our Lady appeared to Bernadette, it was not in a church, not in what we might consider to be a recognized "holy place." Instead, she appeared in a cave by a river. It is God's way of telling us that all life is holy, for he is present in every detail. In the Bible examples abound. Abraham, a wandering nomad, gathered stones and built altars at every stage of his travels (Genesis 12)—his way of saying that the whole world is God's cathedral. The story of Elijah is an even greater reminder of God's involvement in the affairs of humanity, and one strikingly similar to the story of the apparitions. Here again is the cave that in the Bible is a place of refuge from storms and tempests, and above all the place of divine initiative. Elijah, in the midst of a terrible trial, in solitude and distress, takes refuge in a cave on Mount Horeb, the mountain of God. There he is visited by God, who makes his presence known by a light breeze.

In the story of the apparitions, the visit of Mary is heralded by a sound like a rush of wind that awakened Bernadette's attention. Apart from Elijah, other prophets like Amos, Jeremiah, Isaiah and Daniel are further witnesses to God's intervention in the very places and circumstances where their lives unfold. And then there is Moses. Upon approaching the burning bush the voice of the Lord calls to him saying, "the place on which you are standing is holy ground" (Exodus 3:5). The Bible clearly tells us that the ground on which we stand, that is, all the circumstances of our lives, are holy because God is present in every detail of our world.

It is not Bernadette who goes in search of Mary but the Blessed Virgin who looks for Bernadette. She knows to find her collecting firewood near the cave of Massabielle. Here is the image of God searching for his people that we find in the Gospels. Jesus, who meets the disciples, not in the recognized "holy places" of his time, such as the temple or synagogue, but rather in the places where they work, while they are fishing, collecting taxes and so on. He meets them on the roads where they live. And like Mary seeking Bernadette, he is first on the road. The God of Jesus Christ is not some remote impersonal God but one at the very heart of all we do and live. He is the God who eats and drinks with sinners (Luke 7:31–35), supplies the wine for the wedding feast (John 2) and weeps over the death of his friend Lazarus (John 11).

Christianity is not intended as some kind of abstract knowledge "about" God and unrelated to life. It is rather a living with God, a walking with God, a talking with God, a sharing with God, in our actual circumstances. Lourdes is a call for us to rediscover that indeed "the Word was made flesh and dwells among us." We are invited to meet him on the roads where we walk, in the places where we live. We are invited to find him already there searching for us, hoping to share with us the kingdom of his heart.

The presence of Jesus is not confined to the temple or church. It is not limited to the Grotto or to Lourdes. Lourdes simply reminds us that all the ground on which we stand is holy.

In a cave by a river Mary waited for Bernadette. On the roads where we walk Jesus waits for us.

chapter seven

• • • "GO TELL THE PRIESTS TO BUILD A CHURCH…" • • •

*T*hroughout history men and women have built altars and erected temples to their gods. Mosques and synagogues, churches and cathedrals abound. Places of cult and creed, prayer and pilgrimage. The need is universal. We are religious animals. Shrines and holy places mark our history. Lourdes is no exception to the rule. On the site of Massabielle, chapels and basilicas have risen with great regularity.

Was this not the response to the message given by Our Lady to Bernadette during the fifteenth apparition: "Go tell the priests to build a church, and have people come in pilgrimage"? In one sense, yes, but there is more in the message of Mary than just a building. When Bernadette heard these words, she undoubtedly could think only of a chapel in honor of God, and Our Lady did mean this. But today we can hear the message in a different and deeper way. That church is not just a building of bricks and cement. God dwells not only in the temple but also in our hearts. God is not confined to the walls of our church but dwells within the community of men and women. That church, more than a building in God's honor, is the People of God gathered around the person of the Risen Christ. In Mary's message there is a call to build up this community, a community of people who share the life and love of God and witness to that love in the world.

And that message is first given to the priest: "Go tell the priests.…" And Bernadette did—to Father Peyramale, parish priest of Lourdes. And she continues to give Mary's message to the priests of every age, to those who, like Peyramale, are neither the best nor the worst of humanity. The Gospels hide nothing of the human frailty, limits and defects of those Jesus calls to guide his people. It is not the angels (Acts 4:13) to whom Jesus entrusts his church, nor to superhumans, nor to gurus, but to poor men and women "enticed" by God like the prophet (Jeremiah 20:7), sustained by the Spirit and by Mary. It is to such poor men and women that a wonderful vocation is given to shepherd the flock—to be shepherd, acting not as master but as servant, not for themselves but for others, "in the person of Christ." To be shepherd as the Good Shepherd, seeking out men and women in the highways and byways of life to announce the Good News of God's love and compassion, to pardon and heal, restore and give hope, to give the Bread of Life to hungry hearts and reconcile all things in Christ. This is what the priest is called to build.

But it is not only to the priests that the message is addressed. Mary's choice of Bernadette, a simple layperson, reminds us of the vital and important role of the laity—that together we are the church and we are all responsible for it.

What does it mean to be the People of God? Precisely this: that we are to be "of God." That our lives are to be centered on Jesus, on the message of the Gospels. That we are to live a spiritual life, led and guided by the Spirit as we contemplate the mystery of God's love that Jesus reveals. That we are to live as people of the one family, sharing our goods, our burdens and our hearts.

There are many people who come to Lourdes and, before the sick and suffering, are moved to weep. It's a good sign that we still have a heart, but before the problems and pains of life it is not enough to weep. We have to act. Jesus does not call us to be spectators before the dramas of our times, but to play our part, to be active, searching positively for each other's good and welfare. He calls us not to be a people concerned with our own private individual salvation and benefit, but a people concerned for the benefit and salvation of all. We are called to "go and bear fruit," opposing the evil of our time and creating an ever-deeper brotherhood between us.

Today the People of God continue their pilgrimage toward the heavenly city of joy and light. On this journey toward the Promised Land of heaven, new deserts emerge that have to be faced. The new deserts of local, national and international problems include those of the poor, the oppressed and the religious and racially marginalized.

Developing countries with massive debts find themselves in an ever-worsening situation of dependence upon richer nations. Racial discrimination remains a cancer at the heart of humanity. The poor and hungry abound. Even in the United States and Europe entire families barely manage to survive. The "new poor" sleep on benches, on sidewalks, in the subways. The church stands at the side of the poor and humble in the name of solidarity, a new name for charity, as Pope John Paul II rightly called it.

In her Magnificat, Mary proclaims that God "has filled the hungry with good things, / sent the rich away empty" (Luke 1:53). The People of God are called to reflect, in tangible ways, on the image of a God whose preference is for the poor. The kingdom of heaven that Jesus proclaims is not one of self-interest but of sharing our goods with each other for our mutual well-being and to enhance the quality of life, in all areas, for the benefit of humankind.

At the same time, humanity's greatest hunger is that of knowing and experiencing the love of a God who, in the person of Jesus, has come to dwell among us. As People of God, it is for us to give to others in the world that spiritual food for which they hunger, to be that voice "crying in the deserts" of society, the voice that speaks of the dialogue of love God undertakes with humankind.

chapter eight

••• "THE GROTTO WAS MY HEAVEN" •••

"In those days Mary set out and went with haste to a Judean town in the hill country ..." (Luke 1:39). Such are the opening words of the story of the Visitation. Within this Gospel story of a simple act of charity of one cousin for another lies the very essence of the mystery of God's love for humankind and the mystery of our own lives. Mary and Elizabeth meet together in a joy that is immense, a joy that expresses the wonderful design that God has upon them and through them for all humanity.

For years Elizabeth had suffered the humiliation of being sterile. Childlessness amongst the Jewish people was a curse and a great sorrow. Now her shame is taken away. Touched by the Holy Spirit, she is made fertile. She is to bear a child, a child who will grow to become John the Baptist, the herald of the Messiah. Mary, a pious Jewish girl, carried in her heart all the humiliations of her own people—all the poverty, misery and oppression of the Jewish nation. And she held in her heart, too, the hope of a Savior, a Messiah who would come to save his people. Now that Savior was present in her very womb. The message of the Visitation is really the first fruits of the Incarnation itself. God has not abandoned his people to humiliation, evil and misery, but has come to embrace humankind within his own heart.

In 1858 Mary set out again to visit another "hill country," this time that of the Pyrenean Mountains. She sets out to tell Bernadette and the whole world this same gospel message. Within the confines of time and history, within the world of a child's heart, Mary comes to lead us back to the mystery of the Incarnation, to the Gospels, to the Good News that "God is with us" (Matthew 1:23). In the Magnificat, that wonderful song placed on the lips of Mary and found in the Gospel of Luke (1:46–55), Mary proclaims the astounding revelation that God has visited his people, that God has come to favor the poor, to fill the hungry with good things and cast the mighty from their thrones.

"Virgin of Light, you are the smile of a God who loves us." So begins an evening hymn to Mary, frequently sung at Lourdes. To Bernadette she smiles. To Bernadette she reveals the image of the true God. Not that of a remote impersonal power, not that of an angry, tyrannical being who plays capricious games with his people, but that of the God who said "I have observed the misery of my people...I have heard their cry" (Exodus 3:7).

Mary thus reveals to Bernadette more than a smile. She reveals the burning love of God for humankind. The Good News Jesus announced is that the God who gave us life has a name. God is "Father." God is "Love." In his preaching Jesus reveals the "Father" of the parables who searches for us more than we search for him. He reveals God even more in his gestures of pardon, reconciliation and resurrection. Here is a God totally unexpected and unimaginable, not the God of the doctors of the law, the scribes or the Pharisees, who expected a God who reflected their own extreme, severe, judgmental ways.

No, this is the Father of the prodigal, the God of Jesus Christ, who goes out into the highways and byways to invite us to the feast of his kingdom. A God who comes to us, not in pomp and circumstance, but as a beggar of our love.

The apparitions of Massabielle, or the Grotto as it is known today, were for Bernadette the decisive turning point in her life. They happened at a time of humiliation in her life, at a time when she was considered as nothing in the eyes of the world. These encounters with Mary were like an oasis of love and light in the desert of a poor and difficult life. The visit of Mary brought the understanding that God is with us in all things. The Grotto became the high point of her life, not just because of the singular grace of beholding the Blessed Virgin Mary, but also because of the message revealed to her. Her meetings with the Blessed Virgin were an unforgettable experience of ecstasy, wonder and light. They were also the revelation of a message that touched Bernadette deeply, a message of a God so in love with his people. The Grotto became the experience that gave her the strength and courage to continue her pilgrimage through life. In time, as she pondered and understood the words and gestures of the apparitions in an ever-deeper way, she came to understand more fully the mission entrusted to her. Her life's work would be, not just to give the message, but to express it in every way she could in all the daily circumstances of her life. The message of the Grotto led her to develop such an insight into the self-giving love of Jesus on the cross, that her only desire ever after was to share in that selfless love of others. Her spirituality and her life became a generous following of Jesus along the way of the cross, a way of prayer and sacrifice for "her poor brothers, the sinners."

What Bernadette saw and heard at Massabielle remained constantly with her. She treasured it within the very core of her being. "The Grotto was my Heaven,"[1] she said. For there, in the visit of Mary, all the richness of God's love and yearning for our hearts is made known—to feel loved and to love. Here is Bernadette's heaven, the heaven Mary invites us all to possess.

"How glad was my soul, O good Mother,
when I had the grace to look upon you!
How I love to recall those sweet moments
when I was beheld in eyes so full of kindness and mercy....
Yes, gentle Mother, you stooped down to earth
to appear to a mere child and, in spite of her unworthiness,
to communicate certain things to her.

You, the Queen of heaven and earth, wanted to make use of the most fragile thing in the eyes of the world."[2]

part ii

Bernadette

"A broom in the hands of the Virgin Mary"

chapter nine

• • • Every Picture Tells a Story • • •

*M*ost of us, at some point in our lives, have gone to visit a museum or art gallery. Some are very famous places; in Europe you have the British Museum in London, or the Louvre in Paris; in the United States places like the Metropolitan Museum of Art and the Guggenheim in New York City or the Art Institute of Chicago. In these museums and art galleries objects and famous paintings abound. Every picture tells a story, so the saying goes, and generally the saying is true. Every picture does tell a story, a story of the times in which the painting was made, the social conditions, the political atmosphere, the concerns and problems of the era. Portraits tell the story of the people they depict, their fame or notoriety, their history and background. Every picture tells a story and these masterpieces and works of art do just that.

However, there is one portrait you will not find in these famous places—a very simple portrait—the portrait of Bernadette Soubirous. In the art world it will never be considered a masterpiece, but for those who become acquainted with the story of Lourdes this simple little portrait tells a story much deeper and greater than most of the masterpieces of the world put together.

"The eye is the lamp of the body. So, if your eye is healthy, your whole body will be full of light..." (Matthew 6:22). These are the words of Jesus in the Gospels. He speaks of the physical but points to the spiritual. Do we live in light or do we live in darkness? When you look at the simple portrait of Bernadette, you are struck by her eyes. You begin to realize what Jesus means. Her eyes are full of light, not the light that just comes from physically seeing, but a deeper light, an inner light. "For where your treasure is, there your heart will be also" (Matthew 6:21). When we look at the eyes of this fourteen-year-old child, we know where her treasure is. Her eyes tell us she has seen something of heaven here on earth.

In *Forgotten Among the Lilies,* Ronald Rolheiser remarks that much time is spent looking at ourselves in the mirror: "We sometimes scrutinize and examine ourselves. We see the signs of aging; the bags under our eyes, more gray hair.... We all do that. What we need to do is to look ourselves straight in the eyes and see what they tell us. Are they tired, cynical, lifeless?"[1] I agree with Rolheiser. Growing old for a Christian is more about the spirit than it is about the body. We need to recover our sparkle. That's what the Gospels are about. Not to live in darkness but in light, not to grow old through the pressures and illusions of the world but to grow young again in the spirit of God. We need to recover the light in our spirit.

In his song "Candle in the Wind," Elton John memorialized actress Marilyn Monroe (and later adapted the lyrics to Princess Diana). His title was a good description of Monroe's life. She was just like that, a "candle in the wind." She never knew whom to cling to. Many of the people around her were more interested in their own ambitions and advantages than in her welfare. This woman had great difficulty in finding a safe embrace. So the candle burned out. Her life ended suddenly, in tragic circumstances. The flame was already beginning to wane long before her physical death. I imagine that she often found herself in darkness, engulfed by the dark currents around her.

The words of the song were written for Marilyn Monroe, but they can apply to each of us. We are all candles in the wind. The candle is a symbol for each one of us. The light we have as children of God can be easily snuffed out by the darkness of the world around us. This happens when we cling to what is false, to wrong values, to the wrong people. It happens when our ego, our great "I am," replaces the Lord who is. It happens when we cling to the illusory happiness offered by the world. It happens when we prefer to remain blind to the ways of God.

There is an account in Mark's Gospel of Jesus healing a blind man:

> He took the blind man by the hand and led him out of the village; and
> when he had put saliva on his eyes and laid his hands on him, he asked
> him, "Can you see anything?" And the man looked up and said, "I can
> see people, but they look like trees, walking." Then Jesus laid his hands
> on his eyes again; and he looked intently and his sight was restored,
> and he saw everything clearly. (Mark 8:22–26)

Jesus led the man away from the village. Jesus had to take him far from his secure world, his familiar ways, to bring about a healing encounter. It is precisely within this context that we need to hear again Our Lady's invitation to "come here on pilgrimage." The word pilgrimage as used by Mary in the local dialect of Bernadette's time means exactly this: to move outside our own secure, familiar place to meet with others. Mary does not just mean pilgrimage as moving from one place to another place. It is above all an invitation to meet not just others but Another. To follow a deeper movement of the spirit, leaving behind our old usual ways of thinking and acting to come to a personal healing encounter with the Lord. For Jesus himself, his own death and resurrection happened outside the city, outside Jerusalem. Both the gospel message and the message of Lourdes point us in the same direction. We are given a call to quit the familiar and often stagnant paths we follow, to die to the often sinful world we know, the world of illusions and false values, and rise to new life. Our Lady wishes that we leave the ways of our own inner blindness and discover a new vision of life and of love.

In the Gospel story, the blind man was led by Jesus. We cannot heal ourselves. We cannot bring change about by ourselves. We need another to guide us. Mary never points to herself. She always to points to her son. "Do whatever he tells you," she said at Cana (John 2:5). She continues to repeat the same message. We need Another to lead, to guide us, to enable us to see. "Whoever follows me will never walk in darkness but will have the light of life" (John 8:12). The blind man begins to see again, but not instantly. His was a gradual, progressive healing. If we follow Jesus, who is the light of the world, if we commit our lives to his word, then little by little we will recover the sparkle in our hearts. Perhaps our hearts are heavy with many concerns, perhaps broken, perhaps lost. Perhaps there are circumstances that are seemingly impossible to resolve. We need not lose heart. We just need to hold out our hand for another to take. He will take it. He knows that it is our whole being that needs to be healed. If we allow ourselves to be led by the hand of God, all that is heavy in our lives, all that prevents us from following the ways of his kingdom will disappear Little by little the light will come. Gradually the Lord will possess our hearts and transform our circumstances. It is only the vision of this love and the power of his mercy that can give us the courage to see again, to look at the truth, to face what we need to face. All healing, physical as well as spiritual, is given to us so that we may grow under the working of his grace.

Today our eyes see further and our horizons have become wider. The means of knowledge and communication have never been greater. With the highly sophisticated technology we possess, we can explore the wonders of the infinitely small and the infinitely great. Nothing happens on the planet that cannot be communicated almost immediately. But knowing is not necessarily seeing.

For to see, according to the message of Jesus, is to go beyond the appearances, to go beyond the surface. It is to discover what lies hidden at the heart of people and events. It is to look at the visible and see the invisible that surrounds it and sustains it.

To see is to be born anew to the beauty of the world, to contemplate the splendors of the universe, to wonder at the astonishing gifts that people possess.

To see is to discover that God is not remote, absent from the affairs of the world. God is at work among us. God is with us always.

To see is to discover the greatness of God's love for us. "I looked at her all I could," said Bernadette, in speaking of the Blessed Virgin. In beholding, in keeping our eyes on the Lord, we discover what love is, and love, as Shakespeare said, "adds a precious seeing to the eye."

This discovery is never spontaneous. It demands that we allow another to remove the scales from our eyes, to free us from our blindness, to lead us by the hand out of our darkness into the light of new vision and life. "O Jesus, enlighten the inner eyes of my heart,"[2] Bernadette said. As we look at the simple portrait of Bernadette, we see how much his light shines. Yes, every picture tells a story.

chapter ten

• • • "Good for nothing" • • •

"Give me the bread of humility.
Give me the bread of charity,
the bread of seeing you alone in all things
and at all times."[1]

ot everyone, like Our Lady, smiled upon Bernadette. Indeed, Sister Marie-Thérèse Vauzou, Bernadette's novice mistress and future superior general of the order, was heard to say, "If Our Lady wanted to appear on earth, why did she choose to do so to such an ignorant, uneducated little peasant when she could have chosen a holy and well-educated nun?"[2] However wrong the sister was in her assessment of the ways of God, Bernadette would not have disagreed with the assessment of her. In fact, she went far beyond the sister's opinion by describing herself as a "good for nothing."[3] It was in fact a committed belief, a lived experience. She had no great ability or aptitude for anything, neither for the things of heaven nor the things of earth. She couldn't grasp the difficult formulas of the catechism or lessons at school. She remained an ignorant, illiterate peasant. Sickness added to this experience of her own uselessness. And so she was as she said, and experience proclaimed, a "good for nothing."

But to the nun's question, Saint Paul replied that "God chose what is low and despised in the world, things that are not, to reduce to nothing things that are" (1 Corinthians 1:28). Bernadette was a witness to God's choice and preference of the poor, the lowly, the humble of heart. Bernadette was poor in what we consider to be important, but rich in the truly important. She was destitute, uneducated and sick, but she had a heart that understood the essential. She was a "good for nothing" but a "good for nothing" loved by God. And this is the essential!

At Lourdes, God chose someone who, in the eyes of the world, had no value, one of the forgotten of the earth. The arrival of Mary and her appearance to a poor child of no seeming importance, turns upside down the criteria we often use in our assessment of life, and challenges our preconceived opinions about the world. In a world where success and happiness are mostly measured in terms of wealth, power, health, and beauty, Lourdes reminds us of another horizon. Lourdes is the rehabilitation by God of the poor, the humiliated, the oppressed. It is the presence of hope at the center of what seems to be the most useless— sickness, suffering, poverty.

Perhaps what we fear most in life is this: to be considered as good for nothing, useless, inefficient, ignored, rejected, without value. Here lies the importance of Lourdes, for it raises the question, "What value have our lives?" We do not come to Lourdes just for words or ceremonies or processions. In the light of the apparitions and the Gospels, we come to relearn from God the value of our lives

Bernadette becomes a symbol of the poor and lowly of the earth. She reminds us that our value does not come from what we have or how we are, but rather depends upon the free gift of love of Another, that God's love is before all else, that God is not drawn to us by our great intellects, our abilities, our achievements, our success, but by our littleness, our humility. In contrast to the beatitudes of the world stand the beatitudes of the Gospel. Not happy are those who boast in themselves for having it made in this world, but happy are the "poor in spirit...," those who boast in the Lord for having been made in the image of his love and open to the treasures of the kingdom of heaven. It is the happiness of the poor and the humble who, with Mary in the Magnificat, can sing the joy of their hearts, praising the Lord for looking upon them in their "nothingness" and loving them.

The poor are not those who have nothing. They are those who know they have received everything. Indeed, I cannot think of anything that God has neglected for us. Everything has been given. We have a God who leaves all the glory of heaven to dwell among us, who comes himself in littleness and poverty to share our condition and draw near to us. A God who on the cross says, "This is how much you are loved by me," a God who has given us all the sacraments to take care of our every need from birth to death.

Bernadette saw that such a God could only be love and nothing else. That love, by nature, could not remain alone, but had to give itself to share, to restore, to reconcile, to make one. It is the God of Jesus Christ who, looking upon our nothingness, desires to make "the blind receive their sight, the lame walk...the deaf hear, the dead are raised..." (Matthew 11:5).

The sick and all those who come to Lourdes, broken in body and in spirit, are brothers and sisters together on the way of the cross. They tell us of a solidarity greater than that of being sick and oppressed. Like Bernadette, they witness to another solidarity, the solidarity of those whom God has chosen—the weak and the lowly. They witness the oneness of God with the lost, the hopeless and the crucified of the earth. "I was hungry and you gave me food...sick and you took care of me..." (Matthew 25:35, 36).

"Good for nothing?" Experience may say so, but God never will. "I have loved you with an everlasting love" (Jeremiah 31:3b). "I have inscribed you on the palms of my hands" (Isaiah 49:16a). This is the value God places on us. Not because of any merit on our part. Not because of our intelligence or status or wealth or ability. But just because—just because to God it is so!

chapter eleven

••• "JUST A BROOM IN THE HANDS OF THE VIRGIN MARY" •••

he feast of Saint Bernadette is held every year in Lourdes on February 18. A special day, one that evokes a special memory of the first time I celebrated the feast as chaplain. On that particular occasion I had gone to say Mass for a group of people at the Cachot (the old jail that was Bernadette's family home). Afterward I went down to the Grotto to pray and to venerate a relic of Saint Bernadette that is placed on the altar at the Grotto every year on her feast day. One of the workers employed by the shrine to keep the place tidy was there, busy sweeping away leaves from around the altar. He was using one of those old-fashioned brooms, the kind we think of when we hear stories of witches. At a certain moment he left the broom against the altar and went off to busy himself with other things. When he did this, when he left the broom against the altar, I really had to smile. I had to smile at the ways of God's providence for, you see, someone once asked Bernadette if she was a saint, and she replied, "No. I'm not a saint. I'm just a broom in the hands of the Virgin Mary."[1]

"Just a broom in the hands of the Virgin Mary" was Bernadette's description of herself. A simple instrument used by God, used by God to achieve so many great things. Like Mary, she is a handmaid of the Lord. All that God asked of her she did, not just at the time of the apparitions, but throughout her entire life. Bernadette wasn't canonized a saint because she saw Our Lady. She was canonized a saint because she was a saint, because in everything she tried to do the will of God, to fulfill the plan of life God had given her, to do all God had entrusted to her. And this was never more so than as a nun at the convent of Nevers.

Indeed, it was at the convent of Nevers that Bernadette made her significant remark that gave to the broom such a providential and extraordinary meaning. Lourdes had only been the beginning. It is in Nevers, where Bernadette lived until her death at the age of thirty-eight, that her life as a humble religious sister proclaims what it really means to be a servant of the Lord. What to the world was an apparently useless, hidden existence was for Bernadette an experience of the deeper riches of life lived in union with Jesus. As we ponder this union of hearts that was lived out faithfully, lovingly and ever more deeply, within the obscurity of the convent walls, we come to see more clearly than anywhere else all the innocence and docility, tenderness and humility of a true child of God. It is this "little broom" who reveals to us like no other saint the hidden wisdom of the Most High.

Here is the service of the humble and lowly of heart who are supple in God's hands, docile and open to the inspirations of his love. Here is the service of the real poor, not those who have nothing, but those who know they have received everything, that all is a gift from the hands of God. It is the service of those who recognize the presence of Another who is first in their lives, the source of all they have, the promise of all that will be. Bernadette was open to receive all from God, to learn God's ways and to allow God to shape the course of her life.

With Saint Paul she can say that she has done the work the Lord gave her to do (see Acts 20:24). With Jesus she can proclaim, "I have glorified you on earth by finishing the work that you gave me to do" (John 17:4).

Here is the poor humble servant of the Lord who questions and disturbs, provokes and prods consciences blind and indifferent to the ways of God and the deeper meaning of life. Her life demands and urges a radical revision of our quests for power and glory, self-interest and status, applause and adoration. Her docility in the service of God is a constant reminder not to put the Lord at our service but to be at his.

"Just a broom in the hands of the Virgin Mary." Humility and service. The humble heart open to the ways of God, the willing heart ready to do the Lord's bidding. The Lord has a wonderful plan for our lives, just as he did for Bernadette. He calls each of us to play a part in the mission of his love for humankind. Holiness is not just for priests and nuns. Bernadette was a simple layperson chosen by God to be a witness and a prophet of his love in the midst of the world.

"Just a broom in the hands of the Virgin Mary." And what an effective broom she was. What happens in Lourdes today, 150 years after the apparitions, bears witness to the effect of her instrumentality in the hands of God. A call to Bernadette, a call to each one of us to be a broom in the hands of God, to be open to God's designs on our hearts and lives, to be a humble servant in God's work of reconciling the world to himself.

chapter twelve

••• "Oh Mary, My dear Mother, I can't take any more..." •••

Over the years I have come to realize that many pilgrims who come to Lourdes don't really grasp the full significance of Bernadette's life and especially her suffering. Yes, we know that somehow she suffered, but the fact of Mary's appearing seems to them in some way to render that suffering more "acceptable." Certainly, if we focus our attention merely on the apparitions, we can easily make the mistake of seeing the whole story as some kind of fairy tale, like Cinderella being visited by the fairy godmother. The story of Bernadette is no fairy tale. It involves real people whose real lives are shaped, not by the wave of a magic wand, but by a much deeper vision of love. Instead of centering our attention on the apparitions, we have to consider the whole context of Bernadette's life. If we are to grasp her importance for us today, if we are to understand the deeper message of Lourdes and allow this to have an impact on how we think, act and live, then we cannot afford to ignore the great suffering with which she had to contend.

In 1858 life for the Soubirous family was far from easy. A family of six lived in one room, the Cachot. They had no money, no bread and almost no hope. Death and disease were never far from their door. So hungry were they that Bernadette's little brother was found eating candle wax in the parish church during the time of the apparitions. Sharing her family misery, Bernadette had her own sorrows. At school she had to suffer all kinds of humiliation as the dunce of the "paupers' class." She was always sick, a situation that the apparitions did not change. In fact, the apparitions brought an even greater martyrdom. They caused mockery, incomprehension, threats, interrogations and opposition. She had to make the sacrifice of leaving Lourdes and her family for exile in the convent of Nevers.

In the face of trials and suffering we either run or rebel. We become bitter and resentful, venting our anger upon God for all the misfortune that comes our way. We even fear that suffering is a punishment for our sins. I have been guilty of such reaction myself. I'm sure God understands our weakness, our fear and perhaps our cowardice. Even the holy men women of the Bible cried out in anger against God in the midst of their agony.

But this is not Bernadette's way. No complaining, no anger, no bitterness, no rebellion against God. "If God allows it, then you shouldn't complain." Was this an expression of a fatalistic resignation to pain? Not at all. It wasn't that God wanted them to suffer. People in Lourdes could have come to her aid and that of the family. This is what God would have wanted. Just as God wants everyone, in a spirit of fraternity, to take up their responsibilities in order to resolve much of the suffering present in our world today. It wasn't that Bernadette enjoyed suffering. She certainly didn't and stated so quite clearly. "Oh Mary, my dear mother, I can't take any more..." doesn't imply a glorious carrying of the cross.[1] But she followed the way of the cross right to the end as Mary herself had done. She neither runs nor rebels because she is humbly open to Another who in his own death and resurrection has promised that life, not death, has the last word. This is where Bernadette finds her hope and her courage. She believes firmly and deeply in a God who loves her, who truly desires her happiness. What sustained Bernadette in the midst of her trials is found at the heart of the Bible, the promise of God—a promise not for our destruction but for our welfare, not for death but for resurrection.

I have heard priests preaching at Lourdes telling the sick how noble it is to suffer. I cannot understand or accept this. Have they never suffered themselves? How can you tell a mother whose child is horribly mangled and confined to a wheelchair that suffering is noble? Suffering is not noble; it is ugly. Didn't Jesus himself, faced with the passion, not have a sorrow unto death? Jesus didn't come to glorify suffering. He came to glorify his Father's love. If he allows himself to suffer, it is not to tell us how wonderful suffering is, but how wonderful God's love is. If he allows himself to die on the cross, it is for no masochistic intent, but rather to show us to what extent we are precious in his eyes. Jesus didn't come to teach us how to die but how to live. He calls us, not to some fatalistic acceptance of our pain, but to face that pain with him and to allow him to transform our darkness into light through the power of the resurrection.

Bernadette kept on going through her way of the cross, not because of any strength or ability of her own, but rather because of her reliance on Another who never regrets his own creation, on one who pledges himself in our favor in every page of the Gospels. She keeps on going because in her humility she is open to all the promises of Christ. "Come to me, all you that are weary and are carrying heavy burdens…learn from me; for I am gentle and humble in heart…. Do not let your hearts be troubled. Believe in God, believe also in me…. I am the resurrection and the life. Those who believe in me, even though they die, will live" (Matthew 11:28, 29; John 14:1; 11:25).

Our bitterness, resentment and rebellion are the opposite of the man of the Gospels, the man of the Beatitudes. "Blessed are the poor in spirit, for theirs is the kingdom of heaven. Blessed are those who mourn, for they shall be comforted" (Matthew 5:3–4). When Jesus said these words, he didn't intend to glorify suffering. He does not say how happy are those who are poor because they are poor, but rather because to them belongs the kingdom of heaven. He doesn't say happy are those who suffer because they hurt, but because they will be comforted. Our bitterness and resentment prevents us from being open to these promises of God and can enslave us to a form of pride that closes our hearts to a God who is the source and guarantee of what is best for us.

When God freed the Israelites from Egypt, he did not lead them immediately into the Promised Land. Instead, he took them into the desert. God didn't spare them from the difficulties of life. But these difficulties were not designed to crush them. He wanted them to go farther on their journey, to go to a deeper freedom and a greater understanding and trust in his love. Sometimes we are allowed to feel that "desert" experience ourselves—those failings, perplexities and trials that come to us all as we journey through life. With God we needn't give up or run away; with God we can confront our troubles and overcome them in a way that allows us to enter the deeper reality of the Promised Land of his love.

Jesus never said life would be easy. He never made such a promise. What he did promise was, "In the world you face persecution. But take courage; I have conquered the world!" (John 16:33b). Bernadette is a beacon for us of that victory over the trials and tribulations of life. She points the way for each of us toward a more humble and loving confidence in the One who is the giver of life.

chapter thirteen

••• "Happier than a Queen" •••

Blessed the poor in spirit, for theirs is the kingdom of heaven.
Blessed are those who mourn, for they will be comforted.
Blessed are those who hunger and thirst for righteousness,
for they will be filled. (Matthew 5:3, 4, 6)

*C*an we continue to say, "blessed are the poor," when destitution and unemployment touch the lives of millions of people?

Can we continue to say, "blessed are those who hunger," when entire populations suffer from starvation, and justice is continually denied in countries with oppressive regimes?

Can we proclaim the happiness of "those who weep" when war and violence lead to bloodbaths in many countries?

Is Jesus preaching passivity and resignation and pointing to heaven as a panacea for those who find earth insufferable? No, this is not what Jesus preaches. Nor does he want us to focus our attention on the afterlife and ignore the here and now. God may allow certain situations to be. But that does not mean God wants them to be. Much of the suffering we see in the world around us is often the result of humanity's own folly. Much of the injustice, oppression and violence, the denial of basic human rights comes down to our own negligence and crime. That is our sin. We cannot blame God for the cruelty we are quite capable of inflicting upon ourselves. He certainly does not want us to act in this way. What he wants is that we work together in fraternal love in order to create a better world in which mercy, justice and equity prevail and where the dignity and freedom of every human being is promoted and respected. That's what he wants. God gave us the gift of freedom, and he respects that freedom even when we abuse it. We can either create heaven, or we can create hell.

No, Jesus does not preach passivity or resignation. "Love one another as I have loved you," is not a call to passivity. It is a command to give oneself actively and totally for the well-being of everyone else, even to the point of sacrificing one's own life. The Beatitudes, this hymn of happiness, were spoken by Jesus on a mountain in Galilee. It was not merely fine words from a good preacher. He did not remain on the hill after the sermon. He went down from the mountain. He descended to live these words with us in the valley of our own tears and suffering. The beatitudes are a self-portrait. Jesus is the first to live them. It is his life that gives them meaning, his death their value, his Resurrection their victory. They are an expression of his love, a love that is alive and personally engaged. They challenge us to reject the illusions of happiness offered by the world. They challenge us to realize that love is the only true power. They challenge us to trust in a goodness and a life beyond our own.

"Blessed are those who are well-off. Happy are they who have money and comfort. Happy are those who are powerful, the people of influence. Happy are the young and the healthy." These are the beatitudes of the society in which we live today. They are the beatitudes put before us every day in the media, in image and in word. In themselves they can never constitute true happiness. How can we be happy if even one person on the planet suffers? How can we be happy if we have everything and others have nothing? Happiness lies more in the order of giving than getting. It demands that we go beyond the limits of our own self-gratification and smug self-satisfaction. Happiness is not in the power to dominate but in the humility to serve. The kingdoms of this world are about hoarding. The kingdom of heaven is about sharing. Happiness is not seeing how rich we are. It is recognizing how poor we are. That all is a gift. We are not the bosses, just the stewards. Happiness is not the denial of suffering. It is suffering to love, and loving to ease the suffering, and transforming it into new life. This is what Jesus preached, and there is nothing passive here.

Jesus sees a new humanity being born, not in the powerful, the influential or the well-off. He sees a new humanity being born among those who are not eaten up by abundance—in those who suffer, in those starved for justice, in those who struggle for peace, among those who are strong enough to be humble. Those who have their fill and rest content in their plenty cannot hear the cry of the poor. Only those who themselves are poor in heart can struggle to create a better world. Bernadette is one of those poor. She is part of the new humanity Jesus came to create. "I am happier on my sickbed with my crucifix in my hand than a queen upon her throne," she said. She is not happy to be sick. She is not happy to suffer. She said so herself and very clearly. The reason for her happiness lies in what she holds in her hand: not the crucifix itself, but what the cross symbolizes—the embrace of love for all humankind, the victory of love over all suffering, darkness and death. It is the victory of humility over arrogance; the triumph of self-sacrifice over self-seeking; the reign of goodness over evil. Bernadette can remain "happy" for she knows that in her sickness she is loved and held. She knows her sickness can never be terminal. In Jesus, love never dies.

"I do not promise you the happiness of this world but the other,"[1] Our Lady said to Bernadette. This is not happiness for the next life, or the hereafter. It is not happiness promised to Bernadette as a reward in heaven for having suffered so much on earth. No, this is a happiness that comes from God alone and is given to her here and now. It is a share in the happiness won for us by Jesus. We share in that happiness when we, like him, struggle to allow love the victory in all times and in all circumstances.

chapter fourteen

••• "No other gods…" •••

Journalists, as their job demands, are always on the lookout for a good story. That was so in 1858 as it is today. Bernadette was not just a good story. She was a sensational story. A child having visions of the Blessed Virgin Mary had captured the public imagination both in France and elsewhere in Europe. No journalist worth his or her salt could pass up such a golden opportunity. And so the media hounded Bernadette. One French journalist tried to persuade her to go with him to Paris. There, by relating the story of her meetings with the Blessed Virgin, Bernadette could exploit these events to her own advantage and in so doing make herself a lot of money. Bernadette refused. "Money burns me," she said. Other journalists wrote articles about her frequently. Somebody asked her: "How does it feel to have your name in print, to be a star, to be the center of attention?" "I don't know," said Bernadette. "I can't read." Other people made other demands, like asking her to bless religious objects. "I'm not a priest," was Bernadette's reply. These constant incursions into her life can be described as temptations, for that is what they are. They are temptations to power, wealth, success and position.

I find all this very reminiscent of the temptations of Jesus by Satan in the desert. Satan says to Jesus, "Command these stones to become loaves of bread" (Matthew 4:3). In other words, be relevant; turn everything to your own advantage. Satan says to Jesus, "throw yourself down" from the mountain (Matthew 4:6). In other words, be spectacular. Satan says to Jesus, "All these [kingdoms] I will give you" (Matthew 4:9). In other words, be powerful.

Jesus, and Bernadette like him, reject all these temptations and for one reason only. God is the only source of their identity. They live the words of the first commandment: "You shall love the Lord your God with all your heart, and with all your soul, and with all your strength, and with all your mind; and your neighbor as yourself" (Luke 10:27). "[Y]ou shall have no other gods before me" (Deuteronomy 5:7).

"You will have no other gods before you." Bernadette will allow nothing, not money or success or power or anything else to come before God. She was completely poor and could have used the money. She was a nobody and could have used success to her advantage. But she refused to do so. The Lord is first; her trust is in him alone. He will give her a greater treasure than money can buy. She sees that real security is not in wealth or position or power, but placing one's life within the most secure hands of all, those of God. There are no idols in Bernadette's life. She places nothing and no one before God. The Lord is first; the Lord is everything.

"You will have no other gods before you." We may believe we are not prone to idolatry, but if we look closer at our lives, we most certainly are. Idolatry is not about worshiping some statue carved by human hands, like those in Exodus 32 who manufactured the golden calf in the desert of their discontent. Idolatry has deeper and subtler forms. It has deeper and more subtle forms, but the object is always the same: the exaltation of ourselves. This is always the fundamental and dominant temptation: the aspiration of people to be "like God."

To be "like God" is indeed the primordial temptation. We find it in the Genesis accounts of creation, specifically in the story of Adam and Eve being expelled from paradise. In these symbolic accounts of humankind's beginnings, we are given an insight into the true nature of temptation. The Garden of Eden is a symbol of paradise. Here the man and the woman enjoy all the delights of God's love. They live in unity and harmony with each other, and the created world around them. Above all they live in a loving relationship of trust with God. It is a bond of love that carries only one condition: "You shall not eat of the fruit of the tree that is in the middle of the garden, nor shall you touch it, or you shall die" (Genesis 3:3). God's directive is, however, abandoned in favor of personal power. Satan, symbolized by the serpent, enters the scene and sows discontent in the mind of the woman. "You will not die…you will be like God, knowing good and evil," he tells her (Genesis 3:4–5). In other words, he tells her to wise up, to be smart, that God is holding out on them because he doesn't want them to have a knowledge that will enable them to decide life for themselves. He seduces Eve to believe she can have the same power as God, that she can go it alone and no longer needs to kneel before any other greater authority. Eve's sin is one of pride and not of a sexual nature as is sometimes said. Satan was not kicked out of heaven for sins of the flesh but for the sin of pride. It is a sin not of the body but of the spirit, it is a sin of exalting oneself to the detriment of love. Eve shares the sin, and eventually the man with her participates in her wrongdoing. They prefer their own experience and the exaltation of their own intelligence to the covenant of love that united them with God.

Their sin is often our sin. We want to put ourselves first. We want to be independent. We become the criterion of our own salvation. Man saves himself by himself. He can work it out by himself, judge what is right and what is wrong, what is good and what is evil. We eat the forbidden fruit of going our own way and worship the God of our own prideful vision.

"You will have no other gods before you." Idolatry is very much a part of our lives today. What we need to do is recognize it. Notice the exaggerated exaltation of questioning in modern society. Just think of the number of television programs that engage in in-depth analysis. Some people want to appear very intelligent by questioning everything. Today we question and question, but we don't seem to conclude, to reach the truth; there is just interrogation and endless research. Yes, we have an intelligence. It is given by God and is there to be used. But it is there to be used as a humble servant of love and truth and not for inflating our already over-inflated egos. It is to be used in the knowledge that it is not our property but a precious gift given to us by Another and will bear fruit only when guided by his Spirit who will "teach us everything and lead us to the truth" (see John 14:25). To the lawyer who continually questions Jesus as to the means of obtaining eternal life, Jesus replies with the story of the Good Samaritan. The means of finding life is not in the realm of the intellectual, but by moving out from oneself and loving.

Humanity wishes to save itself without God, and hence without love. Humanity claims to save humanity through science, through technology. Modern pseudo-philosophical cult movements such as the New Age movement reveal the same temptation of humanity to exalt itself. However, New Age only leads to old age since it is built on the perennial illusion that a person by himself or herself can save, heal, find peace and find the answers in his or her own heart to the deeper yearnings of the soul. No, we cannot build our own paradise. That is an illusion but one hard to shake off. We still believe that by hoarding up wealth and possessions we will find security and happiness. There is nothing wrong in improving the quality of life. We have a duty to do so. There is, hence, nothing wrong with wealth and possessions in themselves. The problem is how we see them and how we use them. The problem is that they often dictate how we live and dominate our lives rather than the opposite. We put our trust and our hopes in something that is here today and gone tomorrow and fail to realize that our only real identity lies in God, that our true value lies in God's love for us, in our response to that love and not in what we may or may not have. Or we place all our hopes, expectations and dreams on another human being, as if a sinful limited creature like ourselves could ever satisfy all the longings of the human heart.

"My house shall be called a house of prayer";
but you are making it a den of robbers. (Matthew 21:12, 13)

The temple was very important in the life of the Jews. Here was the place where God dwelt among them. It was the symbol of the whole spiritual dimension of their lives. The temple represented the whole Jewish religion. At the time of Jesus it had become empty, without heart. It was no longer the expression of the presence of God. It had become all too human and certainly stagnant. The rabbis of the time had taken the place of God. Their claim to follow God was more outward than inward. Jesus appears on the scene and calls people back to the true sense of the temple: the place of God's presence—and that nothing else can occupy this place. In the Father's house there can be no commerce: Nothing and no one can occupy the place reserved to God alone.

Jesus went even further. He went far beyond what the Jews understood by temple. In another passage of the Gospels he speaks to the Samaritan woman. There had always been a feud between the Jews and the Samaritans over who owned the real temple: Was it on a mountain in Samaria or was it in Jerusalem. The answer Jesus gives points to something deeper. "[T]he hour is coming," he said, "when you will worship the Father…. God is spirit, and those who worship him must worship in spirit and truth" (John 4:21, 24). In other words, we will worship the Father in our hearts. It is the heart that becomes the temple of God. Jesus tells us that we need to build our lives on his presence, that nothing and no one can occupy the first place except God. Not wealth, not possessions or position. Nor can any human being be first in our lives. Not our husband, our wife, our children, our friends. Only the Lord can be Lord. Jesus says, "Whoever loves father or mother more than me is not worthy of me; and whoever loves son or daughter more than me is not worthy of me" (Matthew 10:37). When he says these things, he is not putting before us the choice of two loves. He is not saying to us "father or me, wife or me." He is telling us that there is only one love and that within this one love are found all our other loves. He is telling us that we can only ever say "I love you" to someone if it is rooted within the one who is source of all love.

Without someone greater than we are to give meaning to our little lives, we die in our own illusion. Without a greater love to refer to, we become lost in our own private, limited world. Without another who "ranks ahead" of us, we quickly exalt our own intelligence and follow the blind judgments of our own ego. And when that happens, the bonds of love between God and us are broken. And when the bonds of love are broken, we are in the greatest danger.

It has been decades since the liberation of the Nazi concentration camp at Auschwitz. Television brought the commemoration of events there into our homes. I saw a woman being interviewed some time ago. "It is fifty years since I was here," she said, "but I feel that I have never left. The experience has always been with me." She spoke of the atrocities. At the end of her account she said, "and to think that man is capable of all this!" I can still see her face, the immense pain in her eyes, the voice repeating over and over: "And man is capable of all this!" What man did she mean? The Germans? No doubt. But the meaning is wider. She didn't use the word "Germans." She used the more general term "man." She meant all of us. We are all capable of horrors like this. The Germans were seemingly ordinary people just like us; they were fathers and brothers, they had children and sisters. We can't imagine that we could do to people what they did to the Jews. But we are capable of it. The Nazi extermination of the Jews and others is the most flagrant example of humanity's exaltation of itself. It happens when the only god we believe in is our own ego. It happens when we make ourselves the measure of all. It happens when we have no noble vision of love to sustain us and guide us. Then we wander in the desert of darkness, illusion and self-delusion. In the desert we end up not only "with the wild beasts" (Mark 1:13) but also *as* the wild beasts.

It is in the desert that Jesus is tempted. He allows himself to be tempted. He allows himself to go hungry. By so doing he reveals his desire to identify completely with the human condition. He knows the hungers we have. He knows that in the "desert," the desert of the cold, impersonal world in which we live, the desert of pain and difficulty, the desert of darkness and confusion, Satan comes to seduce us, holding out to us in attractive ways what appears to be the means to secure present and future happiness. Jesus allows himself to be tempted and go hungry to enable us to respond to those temptations as he himself did. His only concern is that we are not seduced to take life into our own hands but to remain firmly within the hands that created us and hold us eternally in an embrace of love. Jesus points us away from humanity's vision of itself to behold God's vision of humanity. It is a vision that indeed proclaims that humanity can become "like God," but not through pride and self-exaltation. We become like God only in the measure that we become as God in Jesus reveals himself to be: that is as the poor, humble, suffering servant of love. Asked if she was a saint, Bernadette replied: "No, I'm not a saint. I'm just a broom in the hands of the Virgin Mary. What do you do with a broom when you have finished using it? You put it away behind the door. That's my place, that's where I'm staying."[1] No self-exaltation. She knows her place. She knows the place of God in her life. She has "no other gods."

chapter fifteen

• • • A VOICE IN THE WILDERNESS • • •

*B*ernadette and Lourdes. Bernadette and Bartrès. Bartrès is a little village near Lourdes. Bernadette was sent there for a few months before the apparitions to live with a woman called Marie Aravant, and to look after the sheep at a nearby farm. In Bartrès was the parish church of St. John the Baptist. It was a place where Bernadette liked to pray. It may seem strange that there could be any relationship between Bernadette and John the Baptist. They are separated by centuries, by geography, by race and by culture. Here are two very different people from two very different worlds. Yet they do have much in common. For both of them are prophets, messengers of God. A prophet is someone who has seen and heard something of heaven and is compelled to speak of it. Both Bernadette and John the Baptist fill the role very well.

John is the "voice of one crying in the wilderness, / Make straight the way of the Lord" (John 1:23). He is the prophet who announces the One who is to come. He is the prophet who reveals the Messiah who is here. The mission of John is to reveal the presence of the Lamb to the world, a presence the world no longer sees. "Here is the Lamb of God who takes away the sin of the world!" (John 1:29). The God of all tenderness and mercy has come to deliver his people from oppression—not the oppression of the Roman Empire or the corrupt religious authorities of the time. His deliverance is of a greater magnitude that spans the whole of history and embraces humankind throughout the ages. His deliverance is from the oppression that lies at the heart of every oppression, that of sin and evil. The God of mercy has heard "the cry of the child in the desert" (see Genesis 21:16), and has come to bring Good News to the poor. Jesus is here to announce a new alliance between God and his people, an alliance made possible and sealed in his own blood, an everlasting alliance of love with the Father. The prophet cries out in the wilderness to open our hearts to this reality, to call us to repent, to change, to welcome Jesus as savior, as the Way, the Truth and the Life.

"A prophet is never accepted in his own country," Jesus said (see Luke 4:24). Many factions did not accept the Baptist in his. As the spokesperson of God, John cried out in the wilderness of his time, not just the physical wilderness that is the desert, but above all in the moral wilderness, the moral lostness of those who had abandoned God and lost the true heart of religion. John opposed the political and religious powers of his day, and they opposed him. They tried to silence his voice, to stifle his cry for a return to the true ways of God.

Throughout history, since John the Baptist, there have been other "voices" crying out in the wilderness. Francis of Assisi, for example, cried out at a time of great corruption in society and in the church, and called for a more authentic living of Christianity. Mother Teresa was the voice of the poor and needy in the wilderness of a cold, hard and impersonal world. Oscar Romero, a Latin American archbishop, sought justice for the poor and oppressed of El Salvador.

Bernadette is another voice that cries out in the wilderness of our times. In a world where a person's value is so often measured by, and dependent upon, financial, material and physical achievement, Bernadette lives poorly, seeking nothing but God's love and her response to that love. She is an example for our time of a deeper vision of life and love. Bernadette sees something of the "invisible" world of heaven. Like John the Baptist she beholds the reality of God's tender love for humankind. She announces the appearance of the Blessed Virgin Mary among us. She reveals Mary's appeal for sinners to convert. To return to the tender ways of God's love. In fulfilling her mission, she is opposed in the wilderness of her times as John the Baptist was in his. The political and ecclesiastical authorities give her a hard time. "My job is just to give you the message," she says. "It is up to you whether you believe it or not." The job of the prophet is always to deliver the message. Bernadette certainly did that. But do we believe, or what do we believe? Perhaps we need to hear again the voice of the child who cries out in the wilderness of our own day. Let us allow Bernadette herself to speak again to each of us in the depths of our own hearts.

"Our Lady chose me because I was the poorest and the most ignorant. The poor are the friends of God,"[1] said Bernadette.

One day, some years ago, I was walking through the streets of Lourdes in the company of a high-ranking church prelate. Suddenly he stopped and said, "Look at this place. It's just a spirituality for peasants." I answered that if I could only be a peasant like Bernadette I would be well pleased. "[T]hank you, Father Lord of heaven and earth, because you have hidden these things from the wise and intelligent and have revealed them to infants" (Luke 10:21).

In choosing Bernadette, God makes it clear that he prefers to place his glory in the hands of those whom the world excludes and ignores. It is to them especially that he entrusts his name and the mystery of his love. It is from the poor, the lowly, the humiliated, those without a voice, that the face of God reveals itself to the world. God is not drawn to us by our greatness. He is drawn to us by our poverty, our littleness, our humility. When Mary proclaims the Magnificat, she does not glorify the Lord because he looks on her as a wonderful person (although we know she is). Instead, Mary glorifies the Lord because "he has looked with favor on the lowliness of his servant" (Luke 1:48). It's in lowliness that we are honored and loved by God. Only the poor of heart can truly welcome Jesus into their lives. Only the poor realize that everything is gift. Only the poor can recognize that Another ranks ahead of them.

"O good mother, you stooped down to earth to appear to a mere child."[2]

"[U]nless you change and become like children, you will never enter the kingdom of heaven." (Matthew 18:3)

Jesus himself is the first to live the reality of these words. He is the almighty God who makes himself little. Consider the infancy narrative of Luke's Gospel. "This will be a sign for you: you will find a child wrapped in bands of cloth and lying in a manger" (2:12). Can this possibly be the sign of God? A child in a manger? There is absolutely nothing spectacular or glorious. Who can possibly go beyond the appearance of a poor child in a manger and recognize that this is Jesus, Son of God? Yet this is the sign of God! The sign of God is here, revealed in poverty, littleness and humility.

"You the Queen of heaven and earth wanted to make use of what is so weak in the eyes of the world," Bernadette said.[3] These words are an appeal for us to discover, as Bernadette herself once did, the depths and hidden riches of those who have no appearance, who are little in the eyes of the world. In discovering the spring at Lourdes, Bernadette has to scrape away the soil. We, too, need to dig below the surface, to look beyond the mere appearance to find the "signs of God" that dwell in our midst. In his book *Followers of Jesus*, Jean Vanier, founder of the L'Arche communities for the disabled, relates an experience he had in India. He was walking down a road. On one side of the road was the most miserable filth and squalor where the poor had set up home. On the other side of the road was a modern seminary with every comfort. "On which side of the road would Jesus live?" asks Jean Vanier. What a question! On which side of the road do we live?

"Hide me, Jesus, in your Sacred Heart."[4]

"Hide" is one of the key words in Bernadette's spirituality. She uses it over and over again. In one sense it is not an escape from the world because she realizes that only by remaining within the heart of Jesus can we truly love and learn to love the world around us. But, in another sense, it is an escape from the world, an escape from a very particular world. It is a flight from that world that sought to confer upon her star status. And to that she is definitely opposed. "He must increase, but I must decrease," she says, quoting the words of John the Baptist (John 3:30). The mission of John is not to proclaim himself but to reveal a presence the world no longer sees. For Bernadette the mission is the same, even if it unfolds in a very different way. It is in her hidden life, her poverty and her humility that she can reveal as no other can the greatness of God's love. I look at the child who, in a life hidden with Jesus behind the convent, touches the lives of millions and leads them to God. This is the voice of one who cries in the wilderness, questioning all our values and pointing us in other directions.

chapter sixteen

• • • THE SONG OF BERNADETTE • • •

*T*here is a story about a famous singer who toured all the towns and villages throughout the country. People flocked to his concerts. One evening he found himself in a village. During his concert the singer asked if anyone had any special requests. An old man spoke up. "Please sir," he said, "would you be so kind as to sing for me 'The Lord Is My Shepherd'? It's my favorite." "Yes I'd be delighted to," said the singer, "but on the condition that you sing it after me." The old man protested, "I'm old and my voice is crackly." But after a while he agreed. The famous singer gave his rendering of "The Lord Is My Shepherd" and the people were captivated by his wonderful voice. Then the old man sang, and the people were even more touched by him. When he finished, the famous singer said to him: "That was wonderful. You know there's a real difference between us. The difference is this: I know the song, but you, sir…well you really know the Shepherd!"

Bernadette certainly knew the song, and she most definitely knew the Shepherd. Knowing the Shepherd lies at the heart of Christianity. This is not academic knowledge. It is not about knowing that Jesus was born in Bethlehem, lived in Nazareth and had twelve apostles. Yes, we need to know all these details, too. But knowing the shepherd is about a deep, personal living relationship, a relationship based on the greatest trust possible that this shepherd is the friend who will never let us down.

The twenty-third psalm is one of the most well-known passages of Scripture. Most people are familiar with it. But are we really? "I shall not want." The words suggest it was written in a time of plenty. But it was not. It was written in a time of want, written by David the shepherd king of Israel at a time when he wanted for everything.

His friends had deserted him, his army had abandoned him, even his own son wanted to kill him and seize the throne of Israel. David was hiding in a cave in fear of his life—that is when he wrote this psalm. It is in this moment of terror, in this great ordeal that David says to himself: Why am I so afraid, why so worried? The Lord is my Shepherd, there is nothing I shall want!

This was a tremendous act of confidence in God. David knows God is able to lead him through this terrible ordeal and restore life, and, of course, God does.

It takes a shepherd to know a shepherd, and David knows his: a shepherd who is true to his name, who will never abandon his flock; a shepherd who will guide us along the right path to bring new life "beside still waters." When Jesus came among us, he revealed himself as this Shepherd. "I am the Good Shepherd," he said. "I know my own and my own know me" (John 10:14). The psalm that David wrote is a hymn of trust and confidence, of courage and hope.

The song of David, the shepherd king of Israel, is also the song of the little shepherdess, the song of Bernadette. She was poor in the material but rich in the essential, hungry for food but filled with love. Sick in body but well in spirit. She was tried and troubled by everyone and everything, but found wanting in nothing. Bernadette, too, knows the Shepherd's heart, the heart of the Lord in whom we "shall not want."

We don't all know the Shepherd's heart. Many come to Lourdes harassed and dejected "like sheep without a shepherd" (Mark 6:34). We struggle with physical sickness and emotional turmoil, with problems of the heart and problems of the soul, with questions of faith and doubts about God. It is not always easy to trust especially in those moments when we seem to want for so much—when told of terminal illness, or suffering the loss of a loved one, enduring the breakup of a marriage, or the death of a son in some faraway, needless war. We do feel harassed and dejected, but we are not without a shepherd. Lourdes reminds us of that. We don't all know the Shepherd's heart, but he knows us. Even when we stop believing in him, he never stops believing in us. Lourdes calls us back to the restful waters of his heart. Remember the words of the song—let them be pondered in your heart:

The LORD is my shepherd, I shall not want.
He makes me lie down in green pastures;
he leads me beside still waters;
he restores my soul.
He leads me in right paths
for his name's sake.

Even though I walk through the darkest valley,
I fear no evil;
for you are with me;
your rod and your staff—
they comfort me.

You prepare a table for me
in the presence of my enemies;
you anoint my head with oil;
my cup overflows.
Surely goodness and mercy shall follow me
all the days of my life.
and I shall dwell in the house of the LORD
my whole life long. (Psalm 23)

This is the song of David, shepherd king of Israel. This is the song of the little shepherdess—the Song of Bernadette!

part iii

Mary

Pilgrim of Pilgrims

chapter seventeen

••• SERVANT OF LOVE •••

On May 12, 1866, just a few weeks before leaving Lourdes to enter the convent of Nevers in the north of France, Bernadette, having acquired a little learning, wrote a very basic account of the apparitions entitled *Journal dedie a la Reine du Ciel* (Journal dedicated to the Queen of Heaven). It was one of the rare occasions when Bernadette referred to Our Lady as Queen. Throughout her religious life she preferred the more intimate and familiar expression, "Oh Mary, my Mother."

In doing so, Bernadette makes no attempt to deny the Queenship of Mary. On the contrary, she points us to where the real essence of Mary's royalty lies: not in the grandeur, opulence and pride that characterize the powers of this world, but in the greatness of a tender maternal love born of God and lived with God. Our Lady is "more a Mother than a Queen" said Saint Thérèse of Lisieux. For Bernadette there is no "more" or "less." Being Queen and Mother are just different ways of expressing the one unique reality of the woman "full of grace." The regal power of Mary finds its highest expression in the humble maternal service of love.

On March 25, 1858, the Feast of the Annunciation, Our Lady revealed her identity to Bernadette. "Would you be so kind as to tell me who you are?" Bernadette asked. The lady smiled. At Bernadette's fourth request, Our Lady stopped smiling, slipped her rosary onto her right arm, joined her hands, raised her eyes to heaven and solemnly said, "I am the Immaculate Conception." To Bernadette it could have been a foreign language. She had no idea what these words meant. As an illiterate peasant, Bernadette had neither the knowledge nor understanding of the dogma of the Immaculate Conception promulgated by Pope Pius IX in

1854. Indeed, as she ran to tell the priest about this revelation, she had to keep repeating the words over and over lest she forget them. This self-revelation of Mary gave greater credibility to Bernadette's story of the apparitions, and acknowledgment to the dogma of 1854. More importantly however, was the fact that, in naming herself as the "Immaculate Conception," Mary revealed more than her privileged position before God. Above all, she tells us that the purest of creatures has not abandoned her children; that the woman conceived without sin never abandons the sinner. To each and to everyone is offered a share in her "fullness of grace," no matter the state of our hearts. Mary is indeed the "Immaculate Conception," the highly favored of God. She wishes to share that favor with we who are sinners; Mary, conceived without sin, is the symbol of a new humanity and wishes to lead all her children to newness of life and love in God. Her deepest way of expressing her immense privilege before God is to be the Servant of Love, and this is where her true identity lies!

In the Gospel story of the raising of Lazarus, two women, two sisters plead for the life of their dead brother. "If only you had been here," they say to Jesus, "my brother would not have died" (John 11:21–23). It is the women who intercede in favor of life. It is the essence of a woman to give life. For a woman close to the cradle, the tomb is insufferable. Martha and Mary plead for Lazarus. They are on the side of life. In Lourdes another woman stands with us and for us on the side of life. It is the "woman blessed among all women." Our Lady intercedes in favor of life, not one life, but the life of the whole of humanity. She is there with us in times of temptation to crush the "head of the serpent." She is there in our times of difficulty when "the wine has run out." She stands at the foot of our every cross, praying and waiting for us to rise again. She is the Queen longing for us to be part of the heavenly kingdom, the Mother longing to enfold all her children within the mantle of her love, especially those who have wandered far from home.

Massabielle, before and during the apparitions, was both the local town rubbish dump and a pigsty. If anyone in the town of Lourdes behaved badly, the locals would say of them, "They must have been brought up at Massabielle." It is to such a place, a place associated with the riff-raff, the lowlife of the times, that Mary comes. In doing so, Our Lady affirms the presence of an often ugly world, often peopled by ugly hearts. But more importantly, she reminds us that Jesus came "to seek out and save what was lost." We do not need to deny the reality of evil either within us or around us. Mary invites us to face it and to transform it. We can break free from our dark ways and grow to the royal stature of true sons and daughters of a heavenly Father. Since the apparitions, being "brought up at Massabielle" takes on new meaning. Our "low life" can be transformed into divine life.

"The child grew and became strong, filled with wisdom; and the favor of God was upon him" (Luke 2:40). Mary wants to bring us up the right way. It was Mary who taught Jesus how to walk, how to speak. She was the one who introduced him to the world around him and made him feel at ease, at home. Certainly Jesus grew up under the influence and guidance of the Holy Spirit. But he also developed his personality under the influence, words and watchful care of Mary. Mary wants to do the same for us and help us grow in the image and ways of Jesus.

September 8 is the feast of the birth of Mary. Once as I stood at a statue of Mary, known in Lourdes as the statue of the Crowned Virgin, a little girl came forward and placed a rose at the foot of the statue saying, "Happy Birthday, Holy Mother." "Grandma, how old is Mary?" she asked. "Oh, hundreds of years old," answered the grandmother. "No, ma'am," I interjected, "Mary is eternally young, eternally young in the fullness of God's love." It was a young Mary who appeared to Bernadette. That youthfulness of being is something Mary would like to share with us all. Conceived without sin, Mary can help us cast off the aging of sin, and regain newness of heart and freshness of spirit.

A Mother, a Queen, blessed among women, Immaculate—Mary is indeed all of these. At the same time she is one of us, a creature. She stands for us, not just in the solidarity of a common humanity, but above all in the humble and passionate service of love.

chapter eighteen

••• Let It Be •••

*W*hen the Beatles recorded the song "Let It Be" in the late 1960s, they must have been reading the Bible. Whether the intention was religious or not, the words can so easily apply to our own Mother Mary, the Blessed Virgin. For Mary does have a great wisdom to give us in times of trouble and darkness and in all the moments of our lives. That wisdom is made transparent in the words "Let it be." "[L]et it be with me according to your word" (Luke 1:38).

Sometimes we think because Mary is the mother of Jesus, the mother of God, queen of heaven and earth, that she sailed through life without a problem. But this is not the Mary of the Gospels. We don't find her in her early life in Nazareth with a crown of twelve stars around her head or with a beautiful white gown and a blue sash and yellow roses on her feet. That's for later. In her earthly life Mary knows problems and pain as we do. There are times when she doesn't understand, doesn't know how it will all work out. There is the real pain of seeing a son misunderstood and opposed; there is the agony of the crucifixion. "[A] sword will pierce your own heart," (see Luke 2:35) and a sword does pierce her heart. What is it that sustains Mary in these agonies of the heart? Elizabeth tells us in the Gospel account of the Visitation: "Blessed is she who believed the promise made her by the Lord would be fulfilled" (see Luke 1:45). Elizabeth reveals to us the true greatness of Mary. She is the woman of faith, the one who truly believes in the Word of God. She is "Blessed among women" because she trusts in the Word of God, in the promises of God. The Word of God does not lie. What God has promised will be so. What God has said will come about. Mary bases her whole life and hope in the word. Whatever the circumstances, whether she is led forward or backward, even into darkness and danger, even into the most agonizing of circumstances, Mary stands upon the Word. It can never let her down. "[L]et it be with me according to your word,"—let everything unfold according to your Word. Mary knows that God is the God of the real, that his plans unfold in the real events and situations we live. She faces that reality with God allowing the word to be her guide, her light and her hope.

We don't always hear that Word. Often communication between God and us is completely disrupted, completely broken down. One of the plagues of our time is noise. We watch a lot of television. It's the age of the image. That's how news and events come our way, not through the written word but through an instant image. The result is that we have no time for reflection, no time to stand back and assess, no time to listen. We are then cluttered up with so much that is unimportant, and God is just drowned out, made absent. At Lourdes Mary speaks to Bernadette. She speaks a word that invites presence, a word that asks for dialogue. Her communication leads to communion. The entire Bible reveals the plans of God for humanity. It is the Word of God that invites presence and dialogue from each of us. It is the word that communicates and desires to lead us to communion with God.

When I was a boy growing up in a predominantly Protestant Scotland, the Bible was considered a rather Protestant affair. Somehow it was not for Catholics. Catholics were limited to more devotional practices like the recitation of prayers. Meditation upon the Word of God was almost unthinkable. In our own times some progress has been made. More is needed. Today we still need to rediscover a more biblical spirituality. Bernadette herself said she "only knew the rosary." But what is the rosary? It is none other than a gospel prayer, a prayer based on the word of God that centers on the main events in the life of Jesus. For too many of us sacred Scripture, the Bible, is merely some written record of the past. We read it as a document that reveals the particular details of a particular people at a particular moment in history. We read it as critics, philosophers, historians or archaeologists. Faith takes us further. Faith demands we meditate on the Word of God as believers. For the believer the Bible is no mere story of past times and forgotten peoples. It is no mere piece of history or archaeology. For the believer it is a living story, a living story for every time and for every people. Above all it is a love story, a story of God's love affair with humanity throughout the ages.

We need to distinguish between the book we call the Bible and God's living word that is addressed to us personally in the actuality of our lives. The Bible is a living word. It is God speaking to us here and now. He speaks to us through Jesus above all, for everything has been brought together in him. We need to listen and not just read. There is no progress in our faith unless we listen to the Word, unless we allow that Word of God to give us a divine outlook on ourselves, on others, on the universe and above all on God. Look at the Blessed Virgin Mary who "treasured all these words and pondered them in her heart" (see Luke 2:19). She gives everything time and space to unfold. Her pondering is not a stumbling in the dark but a quiet confident search for light and for meaning. Mary is the servant of the word, of the Word that became flesh and dwells with people, of the Word that is the Light that has come into the world.

"[L]et it be with me according to your word." We would like to have the faith of Mary. Instead, we are more often like the two pilgrims who find themselves on the road to Emmaus. Like them we are slow to believe. They cannot let it be. They cannot let it be because they stop at the cross. They cannot see the cross as being anything other than an end to their hopes and their dreams. They cannot let it be any other way, for they have forgotten the promise of God. It takes a stranger to remind them, to reawaken their hearts to what the whole of Scripture had proclaimed: "Was it not necessary that the Messiah should suffer these things and then enter into his glory?" (Luke 24:26). Jesus reminds them that the cross is not the end but the victory of love; it is a means of going further.

Shadowlands is a movie about the life of C.S. Lewis, a great Christian author. A professor at Oxford in the 1950s and 1960s, he gave many conferences on suffering but somehow managed to remain immune from it. He had built up a sheltered world of familiar habit and routine. It is only when he falls in love that he begins to move out of his secure, insular lifestyle. And that love costs. It involves sorrow, especially when the woman he loves is diagnosed with terminal cancer. He doesn't deny the sorrow. He enters into it. He embraces it. He suffers to love and love sustains and transforms the sorrow. The movie ends with C.S. Lewis uttering the poignant words: "The boy chose safety, the man chooses suffering. The pain now is part of the happiness then. That's the deal!"

Yes, that's the deal. Sorrow and love are an inseparable part of the journey through life. Cross and glory are part of the one reality. Mostly we believe that we have to separate sorrow and pain because they are the opposite of the happiness for which we yearn. Illness, death, the pains and aches of life have to be eliminated as they appear as an intrusion to happiness. In Jesus we find another way. In him the painful drama of our existence need not be denied. It can be embraced. It can be embraced not out of some masochistic desire to suffer, but out of the realization that from suffering new life can come forth.

Jesus chose the way of the cross not to glorify suffering. He chose that way in order to reveal his Father's love. If Jesus had come among us clothed in magnificence and surrounded by legions of angels, we would have been impressed. We would have recognized a mighty God. But that is about all. It would not really have touched our hearts. But a God who leaves all the security and beauty of heaven, who descends to live with us in our valley of tears and suffering, that is something else. Jesus comes not as the glorious Messiah of the earthly kingdom but as the suffering servant of love. It is only a suffering Jesus hanging on the cross who can reveal to what extent we are loved by the Father. The Father's love for us costs dearly, but he refuses us nothing. The Father's saying yes to love means his own yes to sorrow. As Richard Rohr points out in his book *Radical Grace:* "Through the cross Jesus paid the price, not so that we would not have to, but so that we would in fact know that there is a price for truth and love: everything."[1]

The story of Jesus is the story of every person. Saying yes to love will involve saying yes to sorrow. We need not run away from the terrible agonies that come our way. Jesus asks us to stand firmly on his word as Mary herself did. We can "let it be," not in fatalistic resignation to situations over which we have no control, but according to that word which promises that "he will wipe every tear from their eyes" (Revelation 21:4a). If we stop at suffering, we will be crushed. When we suffer to love, Jesus is there, and he will lead us from the cross to the victory of love. Jesus does not want us to be crushed by suffering. He invites us to trust in the midst of our agony, to abandon ourselves completely to a Father who will never abandon us. "I am the resurrection," Jesus proclaims. I *am*—it is a present reality. Resurrection is not merely about the afterlife. It is for the here and now of our own personal lives. It is the power of the One who has conquered all. It is the promise of never-ending love. It is the promise of never being abandoned to the darkness of our troubled hearts and circumstances. It is the promise that those who suffer to love will find the way to new life and hope.

"Were not our hearts burning within us…while he was opening the scriptures to us?" exclaimed the disciples of Emmaus (Luke 24:32). Jesus did not abandon these poor men to their poor faith. He explains; he opens their eyes to see; he brings back hope and life. So it is for us. He wants to open our eyes by means of his life and his word. What happened in Lourdes happened well over a century ago. Bernadette is long gone. But the memory of Bernadette and the apparitions is still alive. It is not some mere memory of the past, but a memory that sustains and gives life in the present. As we think of Bernadette, of who she was, of how she lived her life, we find much that gives meaning and nourishment to our lives today. So it is with the Word of God. This word is not a dead memory of the past, but a memory that sustains us here and now. It is only the word of God that will bring light in the darkness of our world. It is his word that will help us to create a little more hope in our world, a little more happiness, a little more love.

chapter nineteen

••• Pilgrim of Pilgrims •••

To Bernadette, the poor girl of Lourdes, there appears not a "great Lady" with the airs of a queen, but a young girl, the humble young woman of Nazareth, Bethlehem, Cana and Calvary. When she names herself to Bernadette as the "Immaculate Conception," it is not to bestow grandeur upon herself but rather to give glory to God for the wonder of God's mercy and grace. When she prays the rosary with Bernadette, it is not to draw attention to herself but to ponder in her heart all the gospel, the joyful, sorrowful and glorious mysteries of a life lived walking with Jesus through the events of his life. So she comes to Bernadette, not as royal power, but as pilgrim of pilgrims, the one who has walked with Jesus on a pilgrimage of faith leading all humankind to the heart of a Father's love.

Here is the real Mary. The Mary of the Gospels, Mary who speaks little, who is the first to live the gospel of poverty, the prayer of the heart, the passion of Jesus, the beginning of the pilgrim church.

We have lost sight of her walking the pilgrim's road before us— and with us. We have made her distant. Perhaps we think she is too "royal" to be one of us, too "graced" to be with us. Because Mary is Mother of God, Queen of Heaven and earth, many think that perhaps she was given immunity from the pains and problems of life, immunity from the dark nights of faith common to us all. Yes, she was conceived without sin. But she was not conceived to be without pain and heartache! Yes, she is the mother of the Risen Christ, but she is also the mother of the Crucified One!

At the Annunciation, Mary is given a promise. A promise that she is to be mother of a child, a child to be named Jesus, Savior, Messiah, Holy One, Son of the Most High. What a tremendous moment for Mary and for the whole of humankind. What unimaginable ecstasy must have filled her heart. With such a promise the future seems assured.

Yet it is from that very moment that everything begins to go wrong, and the very promise begins to be questioned. There is "no place for them in the inn" (Luke 2:7); there is no room in Judea. There is no time to feast and fuss over the newborn child, only time to flee with him into Egypt in fear for their lives. The promise is dealt a further blow, a prophetic warning to Mary that "a sword will pierce your own soul" (Luke 2:35), that Jesus will be "opposed" (Luke 2:34). And as he grows into manhood, the prophecy becomes reality. He is opposed. This promised "Son of God" is scorned, misunderstood, opposed, attacked and rejected. Indeed, everything that happens after the Annunciation seems to become a denial of the very promise made her, and humanly speaking a complete denial as Mary stands at the foot of the cross. This Jesus, this promised savior, dies in horrible agony of rejection and crucifixion. It seems the end of the promise.

Mary had no verifiable guarantee that all would be well. She was given no such assurance. Throughout the trials and difficulties she encountered along the road of this pilgrimage with Jesus, she must have asked herself over and over again the same question she had asked of the angel Gabriel, "How can this be...?" (Luke 1:34). What sustains Mary in the dark night of not knowing the real outcome is not some special gift of foreseeing the future, but total faith and confidence in God and absolute surrender to God's Word. What God promises, God will do. "And blessed is she who believed that there would be a fulfillment of what was spoken to her by the Lord" (Luke 1:45). How will this come about? How will things work out? That question comes our way often, especially in those moments of trial and of difficulty that come to all of us. But we can speak about it with Mary and share with her heart, for we know she will understand. She has already traveled the way of the cross before us. She knew the pain of being human. Mary wasn't shielded from the unpleasantness of life. She was aware of the wider social evils in her country. She knew the political oppression of her people. The corrupt practices inherent in society and religion were clearly before her. She knew the heartache of a mother, the agony of seeing her Son rejected and crucified. She is the pilgrim of pilgrims, our hope and our refuge, our courage and confidence, the one who points the way, the way to faith and to trust, to confidence in the promises of God. She points the way to Jesus, that "there is no other name under heaven given among mortals by which we must be saved" (Acts 4:12). She points to him as she did at Cana, reminding us to "Do whatever he tells you" (John 2:5), for his word is of life, of love.

Sometimes our world can seem devoid of life and love, both the global world around us and the personal world within us. We can feel storm-tossed and disconsolate. "When the storm blows," said Saint Bernard, "look to the star called Mary." Before the advent of radar, sailors looked to the stars for guidance. There they would find a course to safety, hope for rescue from the raging storms that had blown them off course. It is Saint Bernard who reminds us that the greatest and the brightest star of humanity is Mary, Star of the Sea, the one who is there when we are blown off course and lost in the storms of life to guide us back to the safe arms of Jesus. This is her only concern: To be a pilgrim of pilgrims, walking with us on the road, leading us to the glorious mystery of God's love.

To Bernadette Mary came, not with the aloof distance of royalty, but in the intimacy of a humble, loving heart, looking at her as "one person looks at another." And she looks upon us with this same humble warmth, as a companion on the same road toward God, as a pilgrim of pilgrims.

part iv

In Bernadette's Footsteps

Walking the Pilgrim Way

chapter twenty

• • • TRAVELING LIGHT • • •

*T*he pilgrimage beckons. We're about to set off on a journey. It's time to pack our bags and get going. It's time to say good-bye. To what? To all and to nothing. To nothing, for the kind of familiar world we leave will always be there, close to us, around us, in us. To all, for the journey is not like any other we have made before. It is a journey in search of God, in search of the divine. Travel as lightly as possible. Excess baggage on a journey like this can be a drawback. That means we have to abandon whatever might hinder the journey, whatever might impede the divine action within us and deflect us from reaching our destination.

Saying good-bye can be a painful experience. It's not easy to say good-bye to the ones we love. For a pilgrim it can even be harder. For the one we need to say good-bye to most of all is our very own self. It's a good-bye to that spirit of independence and self-seeking that desires to go its own way and quickly wanders off the divine path. It's a good-bye to the hurly-burly of our existence. We need to say farewell to frenzy, agitation, to the myriad of voices that invade us. How else will we be able to hear the voice of God speak to the depths of our hearts? It's a good-bye to familiar patterns of life, familiar habits, recognizable landmarks, for we are about to enter unknown territory. "Go from your country and your kindred and your father's house to the land that I will show you" (Genesis 12:1).

Faith demands that we leave our familiar world however comfortable it may be and go in search of the Promised Land of God's love. The experienced traveler knows what to take and what to leave behind.

Experience is a great teacher. But we are not always experienced travel-
ers. Usually we take too much or too little. But this is no ordinary journey. Little by little, as we advance on our way, we will see what we have
to discard. The essential is to set out with a self that's not turned inward
but outward. For God is the Other that we are going to meet. In that
sense, we need to travel light.

Traveling light means we don't have to meet God wearing our
Sunday best, as some pilgrims seem to think. You can recognize them
immediately. They've dressed themselves up in pious airs and saintly
smiles. Wanting to enter the spirit of things, they don another character,
another personality. We dress for the occasion and end up a shadow of
our real selves. And so a kind of saint disembarks with an artificial glow
that you know will never last. Before God we don't need to pretend. We
just need to bring the real and the essential. We come just as we are. That
is the real and the essential. We need to bring our body, our spirit, our
good and our bad, our sinful past and present, our hopes and fears, our
inclinations whether good or evil…everything that is truly ourselves.
God wishes to have a real being before him: one who knows how to
laugh and to cry, one who knows the price of human love and the attrac-
tion of the sexes, one who can turn to him and one who can even resist
him. With God, honesty is always the best policy.

Remember we don't have to climb a mountain to reach the Lord. He
comes to us. That's what the Incarnation means. The Blessed Virgin drew
close to Bernadette. Jesus descended from heaven to draw close to us.

Travel light: "Take nothing for your journey, no staff, nor bag, nor
bread, nor money…" (Luke 9:3). He is not drawn to us with all our
riches and possessions. We don't have to clothe ourselves to hide our
nakedness. We can stand before him in all of our poverty, in all our
lostness. Humility, poverty, littleness are the only passports we need.

They will lead us out of the frontiers of self to meet the Other who waits to meet us.

Travel light. If we take on board everyone else's experiences, we will never make our own. There's always someone who wants to tell us about the wonderful feelings he has had, the great sensations he has felt praying in front of the Grotto. Maybe something special did come his way. All the better. But if we find emptiness and not ecstasy, if we find dryness instead of elation, we must not feel that there is something wrong with us. We are all unique. God speaks to each of us in different ways. Feelings can easily come with the euphoria of the occasion. Faith is made of sterner stuff. "Blessed are those who have not seen and yet have come to believe" (John 20:29). If we are here, it is because the Lord led us to be here. He will not let us leave without some souvenir. We will not go home empty-handed.

There will be guides on the journey. They come in all shapes and forms. Some will be helpful and may enable us to live this moment in a fruitful way. Others will just be happy to fill up our time. As long as we're doing all that duty requires, and following some kind of pious and devotional practices, they will consider it a job done, even if not all that well done. Such guides are not a help. They only serve to stifle the creative power of God's love. Since the end of our journey is God, no one knows the way except the one who comes from God—that is Jesus. While we can listen to the guides, we need to keep our eyes fixed firmly on him for he is "the way, the truth, and the life" (John 14:6). He is the road that Abraham takes in leaving his country toward the Promised Land. He is the pillar of cloud and fire that shows the way forward to the Israelites in the desert. He is the road that leads all men to the Father. We have to follow him—there is no other way. He is the truth that humankind has searched for throughout the ages. What philosophers, thinkers, the learned and the holy men of every religion have glimpsed as truth becomes complete in him. It is Jesus who gives meaning and value to all things. Most importantly, he is life. He is the life that we search for but that often eludes us. He is the life of the spirit, of the body, human and divine life, eternal life. He is the life that only he, who was raised by the Father, can give. In him we find our home, and finding home is vital.

On a television news broadcast covering the aftermath of hurricane Katrina in 2005, some people in New Orleans stood amongst the debris and devastation. Those whose homes lay in ruins said, "We're not moving, whatever the government says. We've come back to live here, for this is home." The whole place was a disaster area, but for them it was home. It held for these people a powerful identity, a radical association. It spoke to them of the roots of their lives, of a familiar world, of precious and loving relationships. This was home! What is our identity, our radical association? Where is home for us? "Your face is my only homeland," said Saint Thérèse of Lisieux, speaking of Jesus. This was not just the perfectly logical and natural consequence of her faith. It was a lived experience. She found Jesus in her life and felt very much at home in his heart. In his heart she felt cared for, considered and cherished. For her Jesus *was* home. That is how it should be for every Christian. We should feel at home in him.

Sadly we can easily become spiritual vagrants. We leave home. We lose our associations, our connectedness and our sense of identity. We lose our way and often end up in a place without meaning, in a place without love. Traveling lightly means getting back on track, finding the way back home. "Have people come in pilgrimage," Our Lady said to Bernadette. People do come, come to "drink at the spring," to be refreshed and to find again in God a place with meaning, a place with love. Pilgrimage is the journey home. Travel light and you will travel far!

chapter twenty-one

••• FOOD FOR THE JOURNEY •••

*W*e find it hard to identify with the saints. They are not like the rest of us. They seem to carry within themselves some kind of immunity from the problems that we lesser mortals are subject to. We think they are given some special grace that makes life easier, more transparent, more manageable. Into that category we place Bernadette. Graced with visions, she had it made. That's how we feel. Her life is steeped in much romantic hype. Everything that happens to her happens in a warm glow. She sailed through life on the waves of a constant God-filled ecstasy.

This is not the real Bernadette. Bernadette was very much part of the real world. Her sickness, her pain, her suffering were real. In Bernadette we touch the wounds. Before the apparitions she was sick, starving and destitute. During the apparitions she was laughed at, misunderstood, opposed and threatened. After the apparitions it doesn't get any easier. Six years after the apparitions, Bernadette left Lourdes to become a nun in the convent of Nevers in the north of France. It must have been one of the most painful moments of her life. Lourdes was a place that meant everything to her, the place where she had grown up. The place that meant home and family, the place that would always mean the apparitions. "The Grotto was my Heaven," she said. Now she had to leave this particular heaven and never return. She had to leave this heaven and embrace another life, another world, another reality.

The journey Bernadette makes is much more than the physical movement from one geographical location to another. It is more than just going from Lourdes to Nevers. She is being asked by God to undertake a journey of faith, to let go of the familiar faces and places. She is to set out on an unknown path, to unknown places, to unknown faces. Bernadette leaves all that is familiar. She enters an unknown, and even at times, hostile environment. The convent was no haven. Bernadette did not have an easy journey through life. Yes, she saw something of heaven, but afterward she had to live like the rest of us in the obscurity of faith. Yes, she had her moments of ecstasy, but only moments. Constant ecstasy is for paradise alone, and Bernadette did not live in paradise. She had to live out her life in the real world, with all its pains and problems, questions and complexities.

With Bernadette we begin to grasp something of the journey of faith that God asks each of us to make through life. New situations arise that can easily turn our familiar world upside down: sudden and serious sickness, the sudden death of a loved one or friend, a marriage breakup, a move to a new job or town, the painful prospect or reality of retirement and so on. Many factors enter our lives and cause crisis. We don't always see the how or the why. We don't know where we are going. Suddenly, nothing is familiar. We find ourselves with nothing to hold onto, adrift in unknown and often hostile territory. At such times our anguish can be great. We cling to fear, anxiety, discouragement, despair or anger. Bernadette points to another way of living these circumstances. Not against God but with God. She decides to make the journey with God, to live the questions, the fears and the anguish with him. She knows God provides food for the journey.

At a troubled moment in Israel's history, we find the prophet Elijah fleeing for his life and taking refuge in the wilderness. Harassed, hounded and humiliated, he just wants to lie down and die. An angel of the Lord appears to him, saying, "Get up and eat, otherwise the journey will be too much for you" (1 Kings 19:7). Nourished and strengthened, Elijah is able to continue his journey and meet God on the mountain of Horeb.

In the troubled times of our existence, when everything feels too much for us, Jesus doesn't want us to lie down and die. He has a food to give us; a food that will strengthen us and give us the energy to make the further inner journey that leads to life. Like Elijah before, Jesus goes into the wilderness. After forty days and nights of fasting, he is hungry. This time it is Satan who disrupts the journey. He tempts Jesus. "If you are the Son of God, command these stones to become loaves of bread" (Matthew 4:3). We know that Jesus will eventually multiply loaves for the multitude following him. But he does not do this for himself. Instead, he replies, "One does not live by bread alone, / but by every word that comes from the mouth of God" (Matthew 4:4). Jesus reveals the importance of the Word of God. This is the food he wants us to have. This is the power of God to build us up.

The Word of Scripture is not some dead record or memory of the past. It is a living Word addressed to each of us personally in the here and now of our everyday existence. When Jesus spoke, he was thinking not just of the people of his own time but of every time. When Jesus spoke, he was thinking about us. He speaks and the blind see, the deaf hear and the lame walk. He speaks and his word heals the sick and the sinner. He speaks and the course of life is changed. The stone rolls away from the tomb and the dead rise again. His word gives life to saddened hearts, troubled spirits and lonely souls. His word is for each of us to bring calm to our anxious storms and light to our darkened hearts. Our job is to listen. Our job is to satisfy our hungry and needy hearts. Our job is to feed on the Word held out to us. This is the first food Jesus offers.

The second is revealed to the people that followed him all day and who had been fed the evening before with miraculous bread. Now Jesus goes beyond the physical to point to the spiritual. He leads the multitude to realize that he alone can satisfy all the hungers of the heart. In the Gospel of John, Jesus reveals himself as the Bread of Life given by the Father to humanity. Jesus is the food of the Eucharist. He is the "living bread," not an abstract God who is far from us, but one who gives us what is vital—his own life. That was brought home to me one Christmas Eve in Lourdes. I was passing by a baker's shop. As I looked through the shop window, I noticed there was a Christmas crib entirely made of bread; the angels, the shepherds, the animals, the figures of Jesus, Mary and Joseph. Everything was made of bread. What could have been more appropriate for Christmas and the child born in Bethlehem— Bethlehem, a Hebrew name that means "house of bread"!

Yes, Jesus came to give himself to us as food, food to nourish and sustain us. He does so every time we celebrate the wonderful sacrament of the Eucharist: "This is my body which is given for you; do this in memory of me" (see Luke 22:19). We are called to feast on the wonder of his presence and the outpouring of his love. Yet we sometimes complain that the Mass is boring. Maybe the priest who celebrates the Eucharist is boring, but never the Eucharist itself. As priests, it is for us to find words that relate the Christian message in a meaningful and relevant way. It is for us to ensure that our celebrations enliven and do not deaden our faith. But, at the same time, we are not at Mass to be entertained. We celebrate the Eucharist to be embraced. Jesus promised to be with us until the end of time (Matthew 28:20). The Eucharist is the reality of that promise; it is the reality of the eternal alliance, the never-ending embrace of God for humankind. That embrace, that alliance, is not something we simply receive; it is something we share. We say that we "receive" communion. The term is badly chosen. It implies passivity that we are on the receiving end of something. The Eucharist is not merely about receiving; it is above all about giving. "Do this in memory of me," is a call to share in the embrace of God's love and a command to actively commit ourselves to personally pledge ourselves to the work of love. A deeper union with the one who is the Bread of Life will nourish and enrich our love.

Jesus reveals a third nourishment. It happens in the presence of the apostles after the meeting with the Samaritan woman. While Jesus spoke with the Samaritan, the apostles went off in search of food. When they returned to the scene, Jesus seemed to have lost all interest in eating. He had been tired, but now they found him refreshed. He was different. He was joyful. And when they offered him food he replied: "My food is to do the will of him who sent me..." (John 4:34). It is the will of the Father that encompasses everything. It is the source and goal of the other foods. And it is in doing the will of the Father that we find life. His will is no barren affair but the loving desire of his heart for our lives. The word of God, the Eucharist, the will of the Father: This is the food that God provides for our journey.

"I am not asking you to take them out of the world, but I ask you to protect them from the evil one" (John 17:15). Yes, we live in the real world, as Bernadette did. Jesus knows it well. He knows the dark forces that exist to disrupt our life and our journey toward his love and his peace. The evil one wants to make us sickly, emaciated beings, people who are underdeveloped. He wants to turn us into menial beings. This is what the evil one wants for us. He wants us to suffer spiritual malnutrition. He wants to inhibit the growth of our spiritual lives by making sure we lack the three forms of food that Jesus wants to give.

The daughter of a miller, familiar with the making of bread, Bernadette knew the necessity of bread for life. As a child of God, she knew the necessity of another more important bread that comes from heaven. "Give me the bread of seeing you in all things and at all times," she prayed. And the Lord gave her that bread. He gave her the daily bread she needed, not just to survive the difficult times, not just to put up with things, but the daily bread of his word and his presence that makes life the precious gift that it is. "Get up and eat, otherwise the journey will be too much for you" (1 Kings 19:7). To be strong, to fight, to endure, to continue, we must eat.

O Jesus, give me
the bread of humility,
the bread of obedience,
the bread of charity,
the bread of melting my will to yours,
the bread of patience in suffering,
the bread of seeing you in all things and at all times.[1]

chapter twenty-two

••• WAITING AT THE WELL •••

One day a woman in Lourdes said to me, "Father, I know some priests have the gift of healing, the gift of the word of knowledge. Do you have these gifts? Do you have a word for me today?" "Yes," I said, "I do have a word for you today. In fact, I have three words: God loves you. If you believe and accept these words, then you will have everything you will ever need!" It may not have been the kind of personal revelation she was looking for, but this is the most personal revelation that anyone can ever be given. "God loves you"—we hear the words but do not always grasp the reality. It is hard to think we are loveable. It's harder still to think we are loveable to God.

Some years ago I attended a healing service led by an eighty-three-year-old American priest, a wonderful man. At the end of the service he said he would bless whatever religious objects people had in their possession. "If you have any rosaries just hold them up," he said. So people held up their rosaries and he blessed them. "If you have any crucifixes, any crosses, just hold up your crosses and I will bless them," he announced. A man sitting in front of me turned to his wife, grabbed her and held her up, shouting out: "This is my cross, Father, bless her!"

Yes, we all have our crosses to bear. The heaviest cross, however, is not really our spouses. The heaviest cross is ourselves. We can be a burden to ourselves. We find it hard to live with our own limitations, our inadequacies and our sin. We can easily despise and torture ourselves. We carry within us the heavy story of our failures and broken relationships. We cling to the mentality that God could never love us in our moral lostness and personal darkness. The poor image of ourselves is made worse by the narrow, mean and ungenerous ideas we have of God. We see him as a disapproving guardian, a stern judge.

Jesus came to remove these false ideas we have of God. He came to reveal a loving Father who is not drawn to us by our greatness but by our nothingness. Instead of despising ourselves for our shortcomings, we can realize that our very darkness, our sinfulness, the world of our broken lives and tortured hearts, is the very place where God is most moved to love us and grant us a compassion that will heal our deeper needs and lead us to better life.

That is what the Samaritan woman discovered as she came to draw water at Jacob's well. In this famous encounter Jesus touched the heart of a troubled woman and opened her life to the possibilities of the kind of love she thought was either long gone or just an empty dream. In five husbands, in five marriages, she had never found a truly safe and committed embrace and a sense of being fulfilled. Now living with another man who is not her husband, she continues to search for that something more that can give her a greater sense of wholeness. The Samaritan woman is a symbol of each of us. We all have broken relationships, failed loves and wounded hearts. We suffer rejection. We suffer self-rejection. Like the Samaritan, we find it hard to believe that anybody can truly love us for ourselves. We long for an authentic love in which our whole being is treasured.

"If you only knew the gift of God...," Jesus tells her (John 4:10). He gives her that gift—the gift of knowing her desire for love is above all the desire for God. He is the deepest answer to the yearnings of her heart. In his love she will find that she is precious, unique and cared for. She will discover that he is the one love who stands at the origin of all our other loves, and within whom all our other loves are to be found and lived. "Our hearts know no rest until they rest in you," said Saint Augustine. He discovered what the Samaritan woman discovered that day at Jacob's well.

The Samaritan woman was far from thinking that someone was waiting for her. It seemed like just another routine day in her life. But something happens. There at the crossroads of her life comes an unexpected and unique experience. Jesus waits for her: "Give me to drink," he asks. At Jacob's well it is the beginning of a new alliance. A Jew could never speak with a Samaritan. They were worlds apart in religion and culture. They were enemies. Jesus removes all the barriers that exist between him and the woman: the barriers of sex, race, nationality, morality and religious beliefs. The Samaritan woman is profoundly touched by him, by his goodness. There is no condemnation, no judgment. There is no hostility, only welcome, only care and concern. Jesus awakens her to the love she craves. He transforms her life.

Like the Samaritan woman we all have our own personal story to tell, and many do come to Lourdes to tell it. They come to lay at the feet of Jesus and Mary all their cares and concerns. In the telling of their story, a surprise awaits them. In telling their story another story unfolds. It is the story of God's love for us. Before his heart, in his eyes, we are never just some anonymous passerby. We are the chosen of God, "blessed...in Christ with every spiritual blessing..." (Ephesians 1:3). As people find themselves at the feet of Mary, perhaps with tears in their eyes, perhaps broken in spirit and in body, perhaps just lost from the rhyme and reason of life, Jesus waits. He waits to meet us as he did the Samaritan woman, to touch our inner wound and heal us, to open our hearts to that world of new possibilities and infinite horizons that is the world of his love.

In many of the basilicas and churches of Lourdes the walls are covered with thanksgiving plaques. They date from the beginning of the shrine right up to the present day. Most are in French. A few are written in English and other languages. What is written on them? Words like "thank you, Lord, for healing my cancer...for freeing me from paralysis...for mending my marriage...," and many more that all carry a story of healing and hope. Although written on stone, they speak of the affairs of the heart, our heart and God's heart. They are a sign of God's love. They acknowledge the gift and the giver. They tell us of the God who is involved in all the stories of our lives.

Jacob's well is always present for us, on all the roads we may have traveled. It is always here and now. It is here in our own personal moment of history that Jesus waits for us. He waits because he loves us. Lourdes is another Jacob's well. Jesus waits not to reproach but to welcome, not to condemn but to save. Jesus waits, waits to invite us back into existence, to tell us again "if you only knew the gift of God."

chapter twenty-three

· · · BAD CATHOLICS · · ·

*T*here are many people who think that the opposite of being Catholic is Protestant. But the opposite of Catholic is not Protestant. Nor is it Anglican, Methodist, Hindu, Muslim or even atheist. Why is that so? It is so because the word *catholic* means "universal," all-embracing, something wide that includes. No, the opposite of Catholic is not Protestant. The opposite of Catholic is being intolerant, narrow-minded, bigoted and judgmental.

In the 1870s the Prussian armies were about to invade France. "Aren't you afraid of the Prussians?" someone asked Bernadette. "No, I'm not afraid of the Prussians," she replied. "I'm only afraid of bad Catholics."[1] Who are these bad Catholics that Bernadette refers to? She doesn't just mean sinners, for she describes herself as a sinner: "Pray for me, a poor sinner," she said. She places herself firmly in the ranks of sinners. So what does she mean by bad Catholics?

Bad Catholics are those who actually consider themselves to be good Catholics. These are the people who outwardly are religious but who have no truly religious heart. They are the people who follow all the religious practices, who know all the correct dogmas and doctrines but whose hearts are far from the ways of God. In our more humble moments, we can recognize ourselves within this group of people that Bernadette denounced. There is a lot of the bad Catholic in each of us. We can easily go to church every day, frequent all the sacraments and have no love and compassion. Outwardly we give all the appearances of being Christian. Inwardly we condemn all those around us. Privately we think we are good. Publicly we make sure that everyone knows the local gossip: That the next-door neighbors are living in sin, that the guy down the street has AIDS, and that the local priest is having some scandalous love affair.

I often meet the bad Catholics in confession. "I live a good life.... I go to Mass every day.... I've really got nothing to tell you..." That's how it begins. I usually answer by telling them that I don't have the faculty for canonization, only for confession! Or they are the ones who never confess their own sin but everyone else's. They quickly excuse themselves or direct attention from themselves by blaming every other agency for their own ills. It is always the fault of someone or something else—the church, society, the world in general. I always direct them to the story of the Pharisee and the tax-collector, for it has much to tell us:

> Two men went up to the temple to pray, one a Pharisee, the other a tax-collector. The Pharisee, standing by himself, was praying thus: "God, I thank you that I am not like other people.... I fast...I give a tenth of all my income." But the tax-collector, standing far off, would not even look up to heaven, but was beating his breast and saying, "God be merciful to me, a sinner!" I tell you, this man went down to his home justified rather than the other; for all who exalt themselves will be humbled, but all who humble themselves will be exalted." (Luke 18:10–14)

The two men start off well. Both begin with God and rightly so. They both put themselves in the presence of God and make their appeal. But why does the prayer of the Pharisee fail and that of the tax-collector succeed? The tax-collector went home "justified."

The Pharisee had followed the right procedures. He had invoked God, but he follows up with an enormous "I." I am this; I am that; I am not like this; I am not like that; "I am not like other men." I am the first, and God is a distant second.

The tax-collector instead touches the heart of God with his humble entreaty: "be merciful." God looks at us with mercy. God looks at us in the pity of love. An understanding touches his heart when he sees our hearts are moved: "a broken and contrite heart, O God, / you will not despise" (Psalm 51:17b–c). The mercy of God is not general or vague. It waits on our cry and has pity. In the presence of God the tax-collector remains small and humble. He knows his place. He is last and God is first. Christian prayer is a rendezvous of love. When we approach God we need to be careful and recognize our place. He is first and we are a very long way behind.

So the parable opens up on a man who does a lot, who is sure of himself and who believes himself right in God's eyes. The parable closes on a man sure about God and is made right in God's eyes only because he knows how to say, "Be merciful." A very good fictional story further enlightens and clarifies.

There is a prophet who is on his way to the mountain to speak with God. Along the road he meets a hobo leaning against a wall. He approaches the hobo and tells him how much God loves him. At this the hobo jumps up and down, dancing with joy. Sometime later the prophet meets a Pharisee along the same road. He tells him also how much God loves him, and the Pharisee, like the hobo before him, also jumps up and down, dancing with joy. Some months later, the prophet goes back up the mountain to converse with God. He inquires about the hobo and the Pharisee. What had become of them? And God answers: "Well, the hobo is with me here in heaven. Sadly the Pharisee is in hell." "But how can that be?" asks the prophet. "I gave them both the same message and both jumped for joy." "Ah, yes," said God, "but the hobo danced with joy because he knew I had remembered him. The Pharisee, on the other hand, danced for joy because he felt he had done everything well!" For the first time in his life the prophet wondered which path he was on: that of heaven or that of hell.

It is a striking story. Which path are we on ourselves? We need to uproot from our hearts the pharisaic belief that we attain salvation by our own efforts. We need to cultivate a more tax-collector heart that recognizes our need to cry out for mercy. We do not recognize our sin because we do not recognize love. When we come to confess our sins, our first task is not an examination of conscience. It is rather an examination of confidence; that we begin by looking at the immense love God holds out to us, and in the light of that love we can examine our own poor lives. It is only when we grasp God's love for us that we can see ourselves as the sinners that we are.

The bad Catholics that Bernadette denounced are those who believe they are always in order before God. Feeling no need of mercy themselves, they can no longer be merciful to others. They are those who proclaim with their lips that Jesus is Lord but in their hearts act as if they are Lord themselves. We are all often like this, and especially when we place ourselves upon the throne in place of God and condemn and judge others.

There are times when we have the right to be angry. We have a right to point out evil and injustice. We have the right to take a stand against evil. But we have no right to allow our anger to lead to condemnation and intolerance. We need to separate the sin from the sinner. When we see ourselves as the sinners that we are, instead of demeaning each other, we can have greater compassion for one another. When we see that, in the eyes of God, none of our lives are in order, but that he loves us just the same, then we can more easily welcome each other into our hearts. Bernadette placed herself in the ranks of the sinners. She gave her whole life for sinners: "O Jesus and Mary, may my consolation in this world be to love you and suffer for sinners."[2] She doesn't react with disgust at the ugliness around her but with compassion. Her concern is not to condemn but to save. There is a passage in Revelation 12 that says that the evil one accuses us night and day before the throne of God. He accuses and condemns. We play his part when we do the same. Jesus came into the world not to condemn but to save. He came with a catholic heart—a heart that is all-embracing, a heart that embraces the whole of sinful humankind. He wants us to live and to love with his heart—a heart that knows it has been remembered in mercy and is ready to render that mercy to others.

Bad Catholics or good? It is for each one of us to answer.

chapter twenty-four

••• "She Looked at Me..." •••

There are looks that wound, despise, kill. Those that frown and bring fear. Those that are full of pride and condescension, that scorn and mock. Those that are full of anger and hatred. Worse still, there is no look at all—just indifference.

But there are other looks, looks that inspire hope and confidence, that cheer up and give new life. Looks of love that appreciate, value— that tell someone, whoever they may be, regardless of color, creed, age, wealth or poverty: You, you mean something to me.

"She looked at me as one person looks at another."[1] Words of wonder, words of joy that well up from the heart of Bernadette as she describes how the Blessed Virgin looked upon her. Perhaps it was the first time in her life she had been really noticed and considered as a unique individual. Maybe the first time she has been seen as a "person," and given such respect, tenderness, and attention.

The eyes of Mary behold her in love, a look of love that invades a child's heart, gives her courage to face every opposition, a confidence to help her compel the priests to build the church, and to be the catalyst for the transformation of a rubbish dump into a shrine where pilgrims come today.

> I remember a summer that I could have lived on the look of love. You know it if you've experienced it. Somehow things that could be a pain or a burden are a joy because you know you're loved. You know your life has a meaning, you know someone loves you...someone out there thinks you're lovable. Just thinking about that and knowing it makes the rest easy to take. The look of love is what each person lives for![2]

How do we look at each other? As strangers, as enemies, as objects, as rivals, or as brothers on the same journey?

Only the "eyes of faith" can help us see the precious gift of life, the precious gift of love.

Only the "eyes of the heart," enlightened by the Spirit, can open us to welcome and embrace each other as People of God, as one family of the same Father.

> Do not fear, for I am with you
> I have called you by your name, you are mine....
> ...[Y]ou are precious in my sight and honored and I love you.
> Do not fear, for I am with you. (Isaiah 4–5)

> As he [Jesus] was setting out on a journey, a man ran up and knelt before him.... Jesus, looking at him, loved him. (Mark 10:17, 21)

So take heart and listen.
As God looked at Mary, as Mary looked at Bernadette,
So God looks at you with love.

> Today you are a pilgrim on a journey through life.
> Sometimes you have to leave your home, your family, your friends,
> to find yourself among unknown faces, in unfamiliar places.
> A little lost, searching for a look, a word,
> a smile, not to feel alone.

> Other pilgrims like you walk the same road of life,
> often entrusting their cares to Mary,
> praying, beseeching, imploring...
> each one with his own story, his own secret.

> God also has a story for you, a secret to share.
> He spoke it through the Prophets, reveals it in Jesus:
> "Do not be afraid for I have redeemed you

I have called you by your name, you are mine.
You are precious in my eyes and I love you.
Do not be afraid, I am with you" (see Isaiah 43:1–5).

"As Jesus set out on a journey,
A man ran up and knelt before him:
Jesus looked steadily at him and loved him" (see Mark 10:17, 20).

So do take heart and listen, for Jesus looks steadily at you and loves
you.

As you pass along the streets of your life
See the poor and the needy around you.
Read the longing in the faces you meet,
for food, for shelter, for warmth
Let the blind help you to see
there is a deeper longing, a deeper need for understanding and care.

See how the goodness of God is written in the eyes of a child,
in the smile of a passerby,
in the hands held out to help and care.
See the Crucified Jesus
in the crosses of those around you.

Look upon your fellow pilgrims
not as strangers, but as brothers and sisters on the same road.
Look upon the sick and handicapped
not as objects to be feared, but as persons to embrace.

Today you are invited
to meet the liberating look of Jesus.
Let yourself be touched by his love.
Think of Jesus looking at Peter...
at the Samaritan woman...

at the one taken in adultery...
Think of how he looked on the sick and the lost.
He forgave all, he healed many.
Do not be afraid.
Recognize your sin and your weakness.

Let yourself be renewed by the God who loves you
and with a new spirit, walk again
on the pilgrimage toward his heart.

If you find yourself in unknown territory
feeling lost and feeling alone
do not think you have been forgotten,
for Mary looks at you "as one person looks at another."

chapter twenty-five

••• A PEASANT'S PRAYER •••

"*O*nly knew the rosary."

"I didn't know the rosary could be such a beautiful prayer. I always thought it was a prayer for peasants." Such was a comment made to me by a pilgrim in Lourdes. I had to remind the person that Bernadette herself was a peasant. That if the rest of the world had a heart half as good as this peasant, then the world would be a much nicer place to live!

How true and wonderful it is that God chooses the weak and the lowly to "shame the wise" (1 Corinthians 1:27). Bernadette, the stupid, the ignorant, the illiterate. The one who cannot "put into her poor head" all the complex doctrines of the catechism. The one who can neither read nor write. Yet here is the one chosen by God to tell the wise and learned of this world of another school where the deeper mysteries of life are to be learned, that of the rosary. This is her peasant's prayer, the school of her heart.

"I thank you, Father, Lord of heaven and earth, because you have hidden these things from the wise and the intelligent and have revealed them to infants" (Matthew 11:25). To a mere child the rosary became a school revealing all the wonders of God's love. The rosary taught Bernadette everything. To read the mystery of God's love for her. To write her response to that love in all the ordinary, everyday events of her life. The rosary was her dictionary, her spelling book, naming and explaining the mysteries of God's kingdom; it was a map guiding her to the heart of God's love for humanity.

The Our Father revealed the Father of all, his coming kingdom, the daily bread of his providence, the forgiveness of our sins.

The Hail Mary revealed a mother, blessed among women, giving Jesus to the world, embracing her and all poor sinners.

The Glory Be, a hymn of praise to the Father, Son and Holy Spirit…the Trinity; a community of love from whom all life comes, in whom life is, to whom life will always be.

The mysteries of the rosary—it is these above all that opened to Bernadette the magnitude of the merciful love of Jesus for humankind. The mysteries are stages of a journey through life. They trace the path of the life that Jesus follows from the annunciation of his birth to his return to heaven. A pilgrimage of faith that Jesus makes in intimacy to the Father, a journey through the desert of the sinful world of humankind toward the Promised Land of his Father's love. It is the way for everyone, the journey, the pilgrimage that we all have to make toward the heart of the living God.

On every step of the journey Jesus makes, Mary is there with him. She is there in the joy of his birth, in Bethlehem, and in his life at Nazareth, in the sorrow of his sufferings and death on the cross. She shares in the glory of his resurrection. It is a journey through life she desires to make also with us. She will be our companion through the joyful and sorrowful moments of our lives and to lead us to the glorious sharing in the mystery of God's love for us. Her only concern is to see us taste, in and through Jesus, the intimate love of a Father's heart.

The custom of saying the rosary as we know it today began in the twelfth century and was approved by Rome in the fifteenth century as an official prayer of the church. It was between the twelfth and fifteenth centuries that the rosary came to be divided into the joyful, sorrowful and glorious mysteries. There are five decades (ten Hail Marys) to each mystery, hence fifty Hail Marys to each. The three groups of fifty correspond to the 150 psalms of the Bible. Thus, the rosary came to be considered as the Psalter of Mary, the prayer book of the poor who could not afford a Bible or could not read. The late Pope John Paul II added the Mysteries of Light to the original mysteries, to include other important events in the life of Jesus, and to make the rosary a fuller "compendium of the Gospel."

The rosary is a simple prayer. It can be said anywhere and everywhere—at home, in the car, out walking or in the hospital. It is a prayer that is said throughout the world. As I pass the beads through my fingers today it is amazing to think that someone else in another part of the world will be doing exactly the same: the pope in the Vatican, a grandmother in Louisiana, a missionary in Africa, a child on a hill in France, a nun in a convent, a sick person in a hospital. The Hail Mary is said in countless tongues, as is the case every evening in Lourdes during the torchlight procession. It is a prayer for every time and every age.

If we really pray the rosary—not saying it in some mechanical, routine way—if we go beyond the mere recitation of words to ponder with Mary the Good News of Jesus, we will begin to expose our hearts to what love is really about.

On the ceiling of the Rosary Basilica in Lourdes there is a mosaic of Our Lady with the French words written underneath "Par Marie a Jesus"—"Through Mary to Jesus." Through Mary the Word became flesh and dwelt among us. Through Mary the rosary can be, as it was for Bernadette, a school where the love of Jesus takes flesh in our lives, a love to enliven and enlighten all the daily events that form the fabric of our existence.

To ponder the mysteries of the rosary, to enroll in the school of Mary, to find there a new understanding of who Jesus is and what he means to us—this is to share the prayer of the poor and the humble, the prayer of the heart, a peasant's prayer.

chapter twenty-six

••• *Ici on Parle Noel*—Christmas Spoken Here •••

*S*ome five million people pass through the shrine of Lourdes every year, people representing most countries in the world. You can see DVDs or listen to audio CDs detailing the story of Lourdes in eighty or so different languages.

As you wander through the town of Lourdes, you will see signs above the shops saying "English spoken here," or "Italian spoken here"— also German, Spanish, Polish, Dutch and so on. One Christmas I was passing by a shop with a sign I had never seen before. It said: *"Ici on parle Noel"*—Christmas spoken here. I went into the shop. I said to the owner, "So, you speak Christmas? Do you speak it fluently?" *"Mais oui mon Pere, c'est le langage de l'amour"*—"But of course, Father, it is the language of love," she replied. Yes, it is the most important language of all. We all need to learn how to speak Christmas.

Many people who come to Lourdes do speak Christmas. Some are actually quite proficient. They speak it when they come to look after the sick and the disabled. When they tend to their every need from morning till night. Others speak it by listening to the pain and troubles of those who come in search of help. Others speak it by spending long moments at the Grotto praying for their loved ones or those who asked to be remembered to Our Lady.

It is what Christmas is all about, for Jesus came into the world to teach us a new language—his language of mercy and compassion. "And the Word was made flesh and lived among us" (John 1:14). It is that

Word we need to embrace and to live, to live in a way that speaks to those around us of the peace, goodness and tenderness of Jesus.

The world in which we live can seem so desperately short of heroes and heroines. But, thank God, there are some in our modern age—people like Mother Teresa of Calcutta, Martin Luther King, Jr., Pope John Paul II, Archbishop Oscar Romero and recent Nobel Peace Prize winner Shirin Ebadi, an Iranian who risked her life to gain human rights in one of the most oppressive regimes in the world. There are many others, less known and famous, who nevertheless live heroic lives and in their own unique way further the cause of love. I have met some of them in Lourdes. I have met some unforgettable characters who are able to speak Christmas fluently and eloquently. Let me mention a few:

Michel from France:

I met Michel near one of the main entrances to the shrine. I saw him, as I passed by, sitting in a wheelchair. He was obviously very ill. I did not really pay him much attention, as wheelchairs and the sick are a common sight in Lourdes. But when, after fifteen minutes, I noticed that Michel was still there, I began to pay attention. I approached him and asked if he was okay. "Yes," he said. I asked him if he was waiting for someone. "No," he said. "But how can that be?" I asked. "Someone must have pushed you here." "No, no one," he said. Then he began to explain. Michel was from the north of France. From his home he had wheeled himself to the railway station, got some help to board a train. In Lourdes he had wheeled himself from the railway station to a hotel, and then proceeded to wheel himself to the shrine. "I'm dying," he told me. "I haven't come here to be healed. I have come to make a pilgrimage for a friend who is suffering great problems. Mary will not refuse my requests." "That's great," I said, "but why are you waiting here?" "Well, you see, when I'm tired I ask Our Lady to help me find someone to push me." "And have you found someone?" I asked. "Yes," he said. "You!"

Father Arcadius from the United States:
He was an American Franciscan who had always wanted to be a great preacher but quickly discovered after ordination that this was not going to be. He was given an administrative job that stifled his deeper longings. He came to Europe and in a moment of prayer discovered that his vocation was to be a pilgrim. He would travel on foot from one shrine to another, taking, in the way of the Gospels, nothing for the journey. He would rely on divine providence for food, shelter, everything. He related a story to me of when he was in Rome. He would eat each day at a soup kitchen with the rest of the poor. One day he found it closed. He wandered in a public park, starving, and praying, "Please, Father, give me today our daily bread." Some time later he came across a plastic bag full of food. He waited a long time before touching it. And finally when he did, he gave thanks to the Father for being such a good provider! At each of the shrines where he stopped (with, of course, permission from his order), he would help with hearing confessions, saying Masses and spending whatever time remained in prayer before the Blessed Sacrament. He was a remarkable man, a true son of Saint Francis, who lived a humble and poor life. He radiated the language of Jesus.

Peter from England:
One day as a procession was about to begin, two cardinals were arguing with each other as to who would lead it. Out of the crowd came Peter, a physically and mentally disabled little boy. He had in his hand a cross that someone had obviously made from joining two branches of a tree together. He went to the head of the procession, held up his cross and beckoned everyone to follow him. They all did, leaving the two bickering cardinals way behind!

Eileen from Ireland:
Eileen was an older woman who lived on her own. "I'm practically blind," she said. "When I get up in the morning, I ask Jesus to take me by

the hand and lead me through the day. He always does, you know. He always sees me through." Eileen was living, like so many I have met, in seemingly impossible situations, yet she had great trust, great hope. She had poor sight but great insight. She firmly believed that her only future was God and secure in God.

These are just a few examples of those who know how to speak Christmas. These characters and stories are really a window to another world, the world of God and goodness. They are stories of self-giving that touch the heart, that inspire, that give hope.

We can all learn to speak Christmas. Jesus will teach us. He will teach us how to speak with tenderness and softer hearts; how to speak words that will befriend the lonely and the lost; how to speak words that will comfort the sad and the grieving. The Word that was made flesh will take on new expression in our lives.

Novena to Our Lady of Lourdes

O Blessed Virgin Mary, on the shores of time you stood, and looked with love upon a poor and lowly peasant girl of Lourdes. A look of love invaded a child's heart and gave her courage and strength to give your message to the world:

a message of prayer and penance,

a message of healing and hope,

a message of a Father's love.

O Blessed Virgin of Lourdes, we come to you in hope and confidence. Watch over us. Help us in our needs. Obtain for us the healing we need, both in heart and in body, and the special favor we now request *(state request here)*.

Our Lady of Lourdes, may your powerful intercession lead us to be refreshed in the living waters that are the mercy and love of the heart of Jesus.

Our Lady of Lourdes, pray for us!

Day One

"I heard a sound like a rush of wind…" O Blessed Virgin Mary, Lourdes began as Pentecost with "a sound like a rush of wind." Help us to live according to the movement of the Holy Spirit in our lives. May the Holy Spirit guide us in all we do and say, and lead us further along the road of God's love.

Our Lady of Lourdes, pray for us!

Day Two

In the name of the Father, Son and Holy Spirit… O Blessed Virgin Mary, your first meeting with Bernadette was marked with the sign of the cross. It is a sign not of defeat but of victory, the victory of love. It is a sign of our Christian life within the Trinity. May our way of living be a witness to this sign, and a triumph of good over evil.
Our Lady of Lourdes, pray for us!

Day Three

"Would you be so kind as to come here…" O Blessed Virgin Mary, we do come to be with you and learn from the school of your love. Help us to "ponder and treasure" with you the word of God, and to allow that word to shape our lives.
Our Lady of Lourdes, pray for us!

Day Four

"Go, drink at the spring and wash yourself there…" O Blessed Virgin Mary, a spring arose in the place you appeared to Bernadette. It was a symbol of Jesus, the living water. Today I find myself thirsty—thirsty for love, for life. Wash away the mud that covers a wounded heart and troubled spirit. Pray that I may be cleansed and renewed in the healing and merciful heart of Jesus.
Our Lady of Lourdes, pray for us!

Day Five

"I looked at her all I could…" O Blessed Virgin Mary, I think of Bernadette's words as I too come to gaze upon you. Help me to behold you in my heart, and to learn from you again the value of my life, and the deeper mystery of God's love for me.
Our Lady of Lourdes, pray for us!

Day Six

"Pray for the conversion of sinners…" O Blessed Virgin Mary, your call is to conversion of heart. Ask your Son to forgive our sin, to heal the wounds of our lostness, to find us in our darkness, and to lead us home to the Father's heart.

Our Lady of Lourdes, pray for us!

Day Seven
"Make of her heart your dwelling place on earth..." O Blessed Virgin Mary, Bernadette urges us to seek refuge and life in your heart. I do so now as I lay before your heart all the cares and concerns of my own. I do so with confidence for I know your heart will embrace mine. I know you are always attentive to the cries of the poor and the afflicted.

Our Lady of Lourdes, pray for us!

Day Eight
"I only knew the rosary..." O Blessed Virgin Mary, Bernadette said the rosary was her only prayer. But it was a prayer that taught her all she needed to know about God and the ways of his love. Help me to pray, and to have a prayer that is constant and faithful.

Our Lady of Lourdes, pray for us!

Day Nine
"Go tell the priests to build a church..." O Blessed Virgin Mary, we are all called to build a holier and better church, a happier and better world. Help us to see the mission God gives us, the part he has called us to play in building his church and his world.

Our Lady of Lourdes, pray for us!

PRAYER TO SAINT BERNADETTE

Saint Bernadette, child of Lourdes and child of Mary,
You said in heaven you would forget no one.
Remember me this day and pray for me
a poor sinner before the heart of God.
Bernadette, you were given the grace
to behold with your eyes the beauty of Mary
and the radiance of her love.
Help us to see in our hearts and lives
the presence of God's love, the tenderness of his care.
Be with us on our pilgrimage through life.
Keep us close to Mary and in her care.
In our time of sickness tend to our needs,
you who were often sick.
In our time of anguish and distress
help us to abandon all into the hands of God.
Be with us at all times to show us the way to "drink at the spring,"
the spring that is the abundance of God's love.
Saint Bernadette, pray for us!

PRAYERS OF SAINT BERNADETTE TO JESUS

O Jesus, give me
the bread of humility,
the bread of obedience,
the bread of charity,
the bread of bending my will to yours,
the bread of patience in suffering,
the bread of seeing you in all things and at all times.[1]

O Jesus, guard me under the banner of your cross.
May the crucifix not just be before my eyes, but in my heart…
May I become as the crucified one, one with him in the Eucharist, in meditating upon his life, in living the most intimate moments of his heart, drawing souls not to myself, but to him who, upon the cross, holds me forever in his love.[2]

Lord, if I cannot shed my blood and give my life for you,
at least I desire to die to all that displeases you;
to sin, to earthly needs, to the desires of my senses,
to the world and to myself.

Cross of my Saviour, holy cross, adorable cross,
In you alone is my strength, my hope and my joy.
You are the tree of life, the mysterious ladder that unites heaven and earth,
and the altar upon which I wish to sacrifice myself in dying with Jesus.[3]

PRAYERS OF SAINT BERNADETTE TO OUR LADY

O Mary, my Mother, be my refuge and my shelter.

Give me peace in the storm. I am tired on the journey.

Let me rest in you. Shelter and protect me...

O Mary, Mother of sorrows, at the foot of the cross you became our mother.

I am a child of your sorrows, a child of Calvary.

Let my heart be united to the cross, to the passion of Jesus Christ,

and teach me not to be afraid of my own trials and crosses.[4]

O Mary, my tender mother,

here is your child who just can't take any more;

see my need and above all my spiritual desolation.

Have pity on me, and let me be with you one day in heaven.

I will do everything for heaven for it is my homeland;

there I will find my Mother in all her glory, and with her will enjoy

the goodness of Jesus himself...

O Mary, my good Mother, may I follow your example

and be generous in all the sacrifices the Lord

will ask of me during the course of my life.

O my Mother, offer me to Jesus.

O my Mother, take my heart and hide it in the heart of Jesus...[5]

1844 January 7: Bernadette was born at the Boly Mill, Lourdes, where the family lived for ten years before they fell on hard times. Her parents were Francois Soubirous and Louise Casterot.
January 9: Bernadette was baptized in the parish church of Lourdes.

1855 Cholera swept through the town of Lourdes. Many died within a few weeks. Bernadette was stricken by the disease and almost died. The effects of the illness left her with asthma for the rest of her life.

1857 Unable to pay the rent, Bernadette's family was forced to take up residence in the Cachot, an old prison that had been abandoned for sanitary reasons in 1824. In that same year Bernadette was sent to a farm in Bartrès, a small neighboring village, to tend sheep and so the family would have one less mouth to feed.

1858 January: Bernadette left Bartrès and rejoined the family at the Cachot.
February 11–July 16: The Blessed Virgin Mary appeared to Bernadette eighteen times at the Grotto of Massabielle (a name which means "old rock" in the local dialect of Lourdes). Today this place is simply known as the Grotto of Lourdes.

1862 January: Bishop Laurence ratified the authenticity of the apparitions of the Blessed Virgin Mary to Bernadette.

1866 July: Bernadette left Lourdes for the convent of St. Gildard in Nevers, a town in the north of France. She took the religious habit and was given the name of Sister Marie-Bernard.

1879 April 16: Bernadette died about 3:00 PM in the infirmary called "Sainte Croix" (Holy Cross).

1933 December 8: Bernadette was canonized a saint on the Feast of the Immaculate Conception.

notes

INTRODUCTION

1. Joseph Bordes, *Lourdes in Bernadette's Footsteps* (Toulouse, France: MSM, 1991).

CHAPTER FOUR

1. Andre Ravier S.J., *Les Ecrits de Sainte Bernadette et sa Voie Spirituelle* (Paris: Lethielleux, 1993), p. 189.

2. Ravier, p. 448.

CHAPTER EIGHT

1. Ravier, p. 216.

2. Ravier, p. 189.

CHAPTER NINE

1. Ronald Rolheiser, *Forgotten Among the Lilies* (London: Hodder & Stoughton, 1990), p. 75.

2. Ravier, p. 349.

CHAPTER TEN

1. Ravier, p. 351.

2. Rene Laurentin, *Vie de Bernadette* (France: Desclee de Brouwer, 1978), p. 222.

3. Ravier, p. 521.

CHAPTER ELEVEN

1. Bordes, p. 47.

CHAPTER TWELVE

1. Ravier, p. 347.

CHAPTER THIRTEEN

1. Bordes, p. 53.

CHAPTER FOURTEEN

1. Bordes, p. 47.

CHAPTER FIFTEEN

1. Ravier, p. 524.

2. Ravier, p. 189.

3. Ravier, p. 189.

4. Ravier, p. 409.

CHAPTER EIGHTEEN

1. Richard Rohr, *Radical Grace* (Cincinnati: St. Anthony Messenger Press, 1993), pp. 144–145.

CHAPTER TWENTY-ONE

1. Ravier, p. 351.

CHAPTER TWENTY-THREE

1. Laurentin, p. 179.

2. Ravier, p. 345.

CHAPTER TWENTY-FOUR

1. Bordes, p. 16.

2. Rohr, p. 44.

PRAYERS

1. Ravier, p. 351.

2. Ravier, p. 353.

3. Ravier, pp. 355–356.

4. Ravier, p. 330.

5. Ravier, p. 347.